BRITAIN'S
FAVOURITE VIEW

Foreword by Sir Trevor McDonald

itv

BRITAIN'S
FAVOURITE VIEW

A VISUAL CELEBRATION OF THE BRITISH LANDSCAPE

Accompanies the major television series

CASSELL ILLUSTRATED

First published in Great Britain in 2007 by Cassell Illustrated,
a division of Octopus Publishing Group Limited,
2–4 Heron Quays, London, E14 4JP

ISBN-10:   1-844-03603-0
ISBN-13:   978-1-84403-603-5

Designed by Roland Codd
Printed in Italy

CONTENTS

FOREWORD

BY SIR TREVOR McDONALD

Britain's Favourite View? Surely it's not possible to reach agreement on that? After all, everyone has their favourites – some iconic, and some with personal, private associations which load even the most bland and unexceptional vistas with precious meaning. So if beauty really is in the eye of the beholder, how are we to reach consensus on a view? Could there ever be a landscape which distilled everything that was special about Britain into one single frame?

Well the answer, of course is probably no. In the Lake District alone there are hundreds – no, thousands – of contenders. In Scotland, the same. But this hasn't stopped us spending a year agonising, arguing and eliminating as we whittled Britain's beauty spots down to the shortlist of sixteen which we would present to the British public, and which are explored here in this wonderful companion to our ITV series.

Believe me, this has been no easy task, and you must forgive us if we have failed you!

But whatever, and wherever, the view, we were always probing for the same things. What were the secret forces that moulded the geometry of the sumptuous lines and shapes displayed before us? Was it - like the Cuillins of Skye – a combination of volcanic might and millennia of evil weather?! Was it – like Hadrian's Wall – a story of ambition and military might? Or was it – like Blackpool – an evocative story of escape from industrial hardship and drudgery?

Behind each of our sixteen views we found different stories, or forgotten characters, and as we delved deeper, we learned that by asking our

'authors' to unlock these histories we could enrich the landscapes in ways we, and they, had never thought possible.

But we learned other things too. We learned how views never stand still; how they evolve, and how – like the Seven Sisters cliffs – they are in a constant process of decay.

We learned how different seasons usher in different moods, turning the Yorkshire Dales from anaemic winter moors to rolling hay-meadows peppered with poppies, and wild flowers.

We learned how passionately our celebrities feel about each of the places they chose, sharing everything with us... from their own childhood memories to the precious insights they gleaned from experts and local residents along the way.

We learned – or had many cruel reminders of – what a fickle mistress the British weather can be when trying to film the ultimate view!

For me, personally, it's been especially fascinating – opening my eyes to corners of Britain I knew only by name or reputation and which I now yearn to revisit and explore. Hopefully, you'll be inspired by this book, and the television series, in a similar way. Hopefully, you'll break new ground as a result of what you've seen, or by what you read there.

The more people enjoy and cherish the special things that we have... the longer they will stay special and cherished.

Sir Trevor McDonald

itself has done more for the region's international profile. Leading artists such as John Creed, Kate Maestri and Andrew Goldsworthy are among those who have contributed to 50 major public works, creating a cultural 'brand' which has reached its apex through the re-development of Gateshead Quayside.

The two outstanding buildings here are Norman Foster's magnificent £70 million Sage Gateshead, which opened in 2004, and the BALTIC art gallery, converted from a landmark 1950s industrial building. The Sage's glass and stainless steel roof embraces two auditoriums for live performances, a rehearsals hall, events complex and 25-room music education centre. Meanwhile, it's exterior profile complements the arches of its near neighbours – the Millennium and Tyne Bridges.

Work on the BALTIC began in 1998 after approval of an ambitious design to retain only the north and south facades. These have been linked by six main floors and three mezzanines together offering 3,000 square metres of gallery space, a cinema, lecture room, artists' studios, library and contemporary art research archive. Since opening in 2002 the building has staged over 40 art exhibitions and received over two million visitors.

Lovers of Tyneside know there is only one place to appreciate the beauty, history, industrial heritage and modern face of Newcastle. Climb to the ninth-floor viewing platform of the BALTIC and look out on a landscape which has been 1,000 years in the making. Day or night, it is a view which does credit to one of the world's greatest cities.

Opposite: *Anthony Gormley's Angel of the North, Gateshead.*
Below left: *The Baltic Flour Mill arts centre.*
Below right: *the Laing Art Gallery with Blue Carpet.*

BLACKPOOL

Presented by David Dickinson

Housewives' favourite David
Dickinson goes back to his
roots to revel in the glory
that was Blackpool, celebrating
its architectural splendour and its
gaiety that brought joy to millions
of working-class people.

FACTORY FORTNIGHT

From Victorian times Blackpool became the epitome of the bucket-and-spade, pint-and-a-paddle, fish-and-chip holiday destination that typified the great British seaside.

The town had miles of sand and bracing sea air of which it was rightly proud. But as it happens those were not the keys to its success. Two factors far distant from the resort and entirely outside the gift of local dignitaries were the reasons behind its atomic rise in public affection.

First was the boom growth of the steam-driven cotton mills of Lancashire, established in the late 18th century as the Industrial Revolution powered ahead. Throughout Victorian times the industry was gaining momentum, and by 1912 an estimated 600,000 workers produced eight billion yards of cloth, most of which was bound for India and the Orient.

The workforce included men, children and a high percentage of women. Although they faced problems a-plenty including disease, shoddy housing and high infant mortality rates, families were at last feeling the benefit of extra income. As tourism became a trend, they often decided to splash their cash on a day out in Blackpool.

And this was only possible with the arrival of the railway. Prior to the age of the train it would take a day to reach Blackpool from Manchester. 'Blackpool Station' opened on 6th June 1853, later to become known as Blackpool Central. In 1900 expansion meant the station had 14 platforms, the same number that presently grace London's Paddington Station.

Only now could Blackpool truly emerge from a commercial chrysalis as the premier working-class holiday venue in the world. By the early 1880s the town clocked up a million visitors a year. The number was three million by 1900, four million by World War I and as many as eight million in the 1930s, when charabancs took over from trains as the transport of choice. No matter that the cotton industry quickly collapsed in the face of cheap foreign imports. The tradition of the Blackpool break had been established.

With the visitors came the innovation of the seaside landlady. Red-brick boarding houses sprang up by the score, usually hosted by a straight-talking, scarf-wearing, slipper-shod bossy and buxom woman whose home was fragrant with fry-ups.

Still, the nation took this stereotype to its heart and the seaside landlady became widely revered. Inevitably they were featured on saucy postcards, a firm favourite among Blackpool holidaymakers from their inception in the early 1930s. Drawn in cartoon style, postcards touched on the taboo but only through artful *double entendre*. At the height of their popularity they were selling at a rate of 16 million a year. One shop alone in Blackpool notched up sales of a million in a year. The business came to its knees in the early Fifties, however, with the arrival of a new government determined to crack down on vulgarity. In 1954 Donald McGill (1875–1962), the artist behind 12,000 designs, was prosecuted under the 1857 Obscene Publications law and fined £50. Postcards were burned by traders fearful of incurring legal reprisals. but when the wind changed and the rules relaxed once more, the saucy postcard enjoyed a revival in the Sixties – though it remains on the backburner today.

Opposite: *Donkey riding along the expanse of sands was one of the rituals that gave Blackpool trippers a holiday to remember.*

BALLROOMS AND BINGO

Every kind of rhythm has been tapped out on the floors of Blackpool's immense ballrooms. First waltzes gave way to tangos, then the foxtrot and quickstep were usurped by jive and rock-and-roll.

The plaster figurines that adorn the inside of the Tower and Empress ballrooms have witnessed all the dance crazes that swept the nation. For what is most remarkable about the surviving ballrooms of Blackpool is their extraordinary interiors, prized for an ornate décor that fell out of favour after the Victorian era.

Behind the exquisite decoration of the Tower Ballroom lies the expertise of one man, Frank Matcham (1854–1920), who was a London architect with a flair for distinctive theatre design. He was responsible for the artwork of the Hackney Empire and the Coliseum in London and the King's Theatre in Glasgow as well as Blackpool's Grand Theatre, opened in 1894, and dubbed 'Matcham's masterpiece'.

His skill lay in the strategic vision he had that combined myriad details such as brassware, glazing, marble, paintings and plasterwork. Even today evidence of his prowess in the Tower Ballroom leaves visitors agape with wonder – it takes a week to clean each of the chandeliers after they are lowered to the floor.

But the Tower Ballroom has another claim to fame: the mighty Wurlitzer organ that emerges through the floor. One of 2,200 built by the Rudolf Wurlitzer Company in New York, it was originally designed as a one-man orchestra to accompany silent movies. The man best remembered for playing it, Reginald 'Mr Blackpool' Dixon, was instrumental in its design – so much so that the Wurlitzer company presented him with a gold watch by way of thanks. It was his bouncy technique on the keyboard that became known as 'the Blackpool sound'.

Indeed the music of the ballroom became familiar to many in post-war Britain via radio shows broadcast from there. And it became a well loved sight with its typically Victorian interior, being the venue on numerous occasions for television's initial *Come Dancing* series, which ran between 1949 and 1998.

Sharp-eyed visitors can see the inscription on the ballroom wall. 'Bid me discourse, I will enchant thine ear,' from *Venus and Adonis*, one of Shakespeare's sonnets.

Although similar in flavour, the Empress Ballroom is the handiwork of a different company. Opened in 1897, the ballroom is part of the Winter Gardens complex that also includes an opera house, a theatre and other luxuriously appointed venues across a 6-acre site. A 67 metre (220 ft) ferris wheel with carriages that could carry 30 people attached to the Winter Gardens has long gone. But the Empress Ballroom with its boxes and its sprung floor, goes on and on. It's now just as likely to be the venue for a pop concert as a dance, and has hosted some of today's biggest stars. That Blackpool could support at least two immense ballrooms – alongside other smaller venues – indicates just how popular dancing once was.

Bingo didn't arrive in Britain until 1960 when a change in the gaming laws gave it the green light. *Come Dancing* creator Eric Morley, of the Mecca group, introduced the game from Italy via the US, and it became popular in cavernous theatres left empty after the arrival of domestic television.

Opposite: *Extraordinary ornamentation at the Tower Ballroom has added grandeur to dance events through the modern era.*

ILLUMINATIONS

It began in 1879 with eight arc lights, creating a phenomenon called 'artificial sunshine'. Darkness becomes day, to the disbelieving eyes of a thronging crowd.

At the time this was cutting-edge technology. After all, Thomas Edison did not apply for a patent related to his invention of the modern electric light bulb until 1880. So, in 1879, an astonishing 70,000 people travelled to Blackpool for the spectacle.

But little did the pioneers of Blackpool's illuminations know they were at the start of something big. Nearly 130 years later it's the honeypot hotspot of the Northwest, a 'must-see' annual attraction for millions of families. For 66 days the darkening autumn skies above the Irish Sea resort are charged with twinkling, shape-shifting lights of every conceivable colour along a 10-km (6-mile) stretch of coastline.

And the illuminations are still pushing back the boundaries of technology. It's not just light bulbs – although there are thousands of those, about 100 of which cling to Blackpool Tower's flagpole alone – but there are also fibreoptics, lasers and LED lights.

It costs nearly £2.5 million to stage, costing £50,000 in electricity consumption alone. The cable and wiring needed for the displays run for 320 km (200 miles).

But it hasn't always been plain sailing. As early as 1912 there were 10,000 bulbs gracing the town to mark a royal visit – but the lights frequently went out when – with an incoming tide – seawater seeped into the cast-iron wiring pipes.

Lighting designers raised the bar in 1939, producing what townspeople presumed to be the best-ever display. The day after it was previewed World War II broke out, and the plug was pulled as part of a nationwide blackout.

After the war the tradition of inviting a celebrity to switch on the illuminations began. Among those who have assumed the honour are entertainer George Formby, the cast of TV sitcom *Dad's Army* and Kermit the Frog, accompanied by other muppets. In 1955 as the Cold War raged in earnest following the Korean conflict, Blackpool risked political flak by asking controversial Soviet ambassador Jacob Malik to preside at the ceremony.

Incorporated in the illuminations the town's trams are also festooned with lights. The trams, familiar year-round for their high wires, soft lines and clicking purr, ferry tourists to destinations along the Golden Mile and beyond. Blackpool was the first place in Britain to install a tram system in 1885, and a single carriage from the original running stock has been preserved for posterity. Alongside the illuminations, it is probably tram travel that typifies for most a trip to Blackpool.

As for the Golden Mile, well, it's not so named for the accuracy of its measurements but, for the colour of the money that's generated along its pavements. This is the heart of commercial Blackpool, where candy floss and 'kiss-me-quick' hats have given way to slot machines. Established in 1897, it's hard to imagine that any of Blackpool's millions of annual visitors leave without trying their luck on the one-armed bandits in the hope of being rewarded by the crash of cash. It is perhaps here that Blackpool best earns its reputation as the 'Las Vegas' of Lancashire.

Opposite, above left and right: *During autumn nights Blackpool is bathed in a golden glow after the ever-expanding illuminations are fired up.*

BLACKPOOL TOWER

Scanning the prom your eye is irresistibly drawn to the world-famous Blackpool Tower. It prods the skyline above the beach, the icon known to all as the Northwest's pleasure dome.

Blackpool Tower is a second cousin of the Eiffel Tower in France. It was built in 1894, seven years after the famous framework in Paris – at the time the tallest building in the world. Although Blackpool's tower is a shade under half its height, both enjoy similar sleek lines and graceful girders.

Despite its more diminutive stature – Blackpool Tower stands 158 m (518 ft 9 ins) tall, about the same as the spires of Cologne Cathedral in Germany – the view from the top is nonetheless breathtaking. On a clear day it's possible to see as far as 42 km (26 miles) distant, which encompasses acres of Lancashire, the Isle of Man, North Wales and the lower reaches of Cumbria. More immediately, you can see the ground below through a 5 cm (2 in) thick laminated glass floor.

It's all the more thrilling on a windy day when it's possible to detect a slight sway in the red-painted structure. The route to four viewing platforms at the top is by two lifts that make at least 50,000 trips a year except for those involved in Tower maintenance. 'Stick men', as the caretakers are called, use ladders.

The Tower has always been so central to the resort that until 1946 its telephone number was Blackpool 1. Three years later it was struck by lightning – and the dramatic moment was captured in a photograph.

However, the Tower is more than just a panoramic viewpoint. Its vital statistics alone are impressive. It weighs 2,586 tons, initially cost £42,000 to build, it was rebuilt in the early 1900s after lack of maintenance took its toll and at first it cost visitors just sixpence to get to the top. It takes seven years to paint the Tower from top to bottom.

But what lies beneath is also of interest for, unlike its French counterpart, the tower rises out of a stout building that houses a circus, a ballroom and an aquarium. Once the site of Dr Cocker's Menagerie in the late 1870s, the aquarium containing 57 species occupies the oldest corner of the complex. Among the inhabitants of its 17 tanks are piranha fish that are more than 30 years old.

The animal-free circus sits squarely between the tower's feet and is probably the only one in the world to take place under glorious gilt ceilings. Prior to making the big time in Hollywood, W. C. Fields (1880–1966) was a clown for a season in the circus, before the start of World War I. On the other hand, Italian-born Charlie Cairoli was a fixture for 39 years, winning the hearts of children across the nation.

The Tower is also the home of its silver replica, presented to Sir John Bickerstaffe whose brainchild it was. Apart from a dynamic focus for the tourist trade, his legacy to Blackpool upon his death in 1930 included the silver model, to be kept within its structure forever.

Opposite: *With its dark iron struts silhouetted against a clear blue sky, Blackpool Tower pinpoints the beating heart of the resort.*

ALL'S FAIR IN BLACKPOOL'S PLEASURE BEACH

Among the millions who flock to Blackpool every year there is a significant number of adrenalin junkies, who travel for miles to sample the white-knuckle rides sited on the Pleasure Beach, Blackpool.

The fairground was established two years after the Tower and was the most popular tourist attraction in Britain in 2006, bringing some six million visitors through its gates.

Founder William George Bean intended to create '...an American Style Amusement Park, the fundamental principle of which is to make adults feel like children again and to inspire gaiety of a primarily innocent character.'

Bean then bought 17 hectares (42 acres) of prime seafront to bring his dream to life, and it is here that the sought-after rides of the Pleasure Beach stand shoulder to shoulder today.

Among today's favourites are the Pepsi Max Big One, which opened in 1994 at a cost of £12 million and was for a while the tallest roller coaster in the world, and Bling, a 2004 addition with a £2 million price tag. Perhaps the most famous is Valhalla, a covered Viking-themed water ride that marked the park's entry into the new millennium at a jaw-dropping £15 million. The rides are designed primarily for those who feel a need for speed, who believe that g-force tugging at their cheeks is the hallmark of a great holiday.

But some nostalgically-minded folk come here to see Blackpool's five wooden roller coasters in action, the most that are gathered together anywhere in the world. The biggest hit among these old-timers is usually the Big Dipper, installed in 1923 with revolutionary 'upstop' wheels and extended 13 years later to its present size of 1,100 m (3,300 ft) in length travelling at heights of up to 20 m (60 ft). The last remnants of the original were destroyed by fire during the Fifties. It has majestic arcs, plunging gradients and gives riders – especially those at the back – plenty of 'air-time', that is, moments when fresh-air separates bottom and seat.

Indeed American teacher Richard Rodriguez is so taken with this particular 'woodie' that he is prone to riding it for days and weeks at a time. His first record of nearly 23 days riding non stop in the Big Dipper set in 1994 now seems tame. He is breaking his own record all the time, but at the last count he was confined to the carriage for more than three months, covering a distance that equated to a return trip to Australia.

The Big Dipper has attracted other record breakers. In 2003 a group of 32 pensioners with an average age of 75 and a total age of 2,408 became the world's oldest roller coaster riders.

Other riders are keen to experience the ghost train, said to be haunted by 'Cloggy', a former employee so named for his footwear.

Not all rides stay the same. The once-popular log flume has recently been dismantled to make way for a different attraction and construction workers excavating the lake beneath claimed to have found Marlene Dietrich's earring. The Hollywood star apparently lost it during a visit, according to letters kept by the then owner. They also discovered 35 keys, three sets of false teeth, 13 pairs of glasses, a wig, a bra and a glass eye.

Opposite: *High and mighty, the rides at Blackpool's Pleasure Beach pull in thousands of thrill seekers each year, especially this one, the Pepsi Max Big One Roller Coaster.*

PIERS

With visitor numbers booming and the local economy in tip-top form, Blackpool's great and good felt they could walk on water. To ensure it was so, they invested in pier-building.

The North Pier came first, measuring 500 m (1,500 ft). Built in 1863, it complemented the newly opened railway station, beckoning passengers directly to the sea front. Initially it was simply called the Blackpool Pier as, for a short while, it stood alone.

During subsequent decades new wings and jetties were added, although sporadic fires tended to counter the expansions. It is one of nine piers left in Britain to boast a theatre for 'end-of-the-pier' entertainment.

In 1897 the pier was badly damaged when a gale drove the moored training ship HMS *Foudroyant* into the structure. The vessel, launched in 1798, had once been

Nelson's flagship. In a bid to recover some cash from the disaster the salvagers generated a trade from souvenirs made from the ship's wood and ironwork, including furniture and walking sticks.

The pier was a popular concept, so much so that planning for another began almost immediately. It opened in 1868 and measured 336 m (1,000 ft), benefiting from construction techniques that had been honed just a short distance up the beach. It was such a success that within a decade much of the woodwork was replaced with more durable iron. Initially called South Jetty, it was thought it would satisfy an increasing

demand for steamer excursions to locations including Cumbria, the Isle of Man and Southport. Yet it became better known for dancing. For a long time the toe-tapping took place in the open air until the perils of Blackpool's climate forced dancers inside.

It was later renamed Central Pier and interest has been revived following the arrival of a ferris wheel. It's at least 100 ft (30.95 m) high with 26 cars. Before the attraction was installed, pier reinforcement work costing £250,000 was carried out.

Still it was deemed Blackpool could cope with another pier. In 1893 the Victoria Pier was opened, shorter and stouter than the others but able to accommodate 36 shops, a bandstand, a photographic stall and the immense Grand Pavilion theatre, with 3,000 seats.

Later called South Pier this was unashamedly aimed at genteel tourists seeking to escape some of the vulgar aspects of the resort. Its brief was for 'high-class vocal and instrumental concerts, variety, entertainment, military and other band contests.' Thus the piers became emblematic of the class divide that dominated in Britain during Blackpool's heyday. It was nearly destroyed by fire on two occasions, in 1958 and 1964, but renovation assured its future.

The view from the end of the piers brings together old and new in a town that has Sir Hiram Maxim's Captive Flying Machine fairground ride, dating from 1904, alongside Infusion, the latest word for loop-and-roll thrill-seekers. Trippers can visit a swimming pool with all the latest whistles and bells in water design using a historic tram system. Blackpool, its motto: 'Progress', keeps one eye on the future while watching carefully over its illustrious past.

Above: *Rivulets and sticky sand, an elegant walkway has given millions the opportunity to stroll at the seaside in clean comfort and get the best of the bracing sea air.*

SEVEN SISTERS

Presented by Des Lynam

Broadcaster Des Lynam enjoys the
varied landscapes beginning from
his home town of Brighton – where
hedonism rests alongside tradition --
to Beachy Head and the white cliffs
of the Seven Sisters.

REGENCY BRIGHTON

Once it was a fishing village surrounded by farms and threatened by an uncertain tide and excitable foreign ships. Then along came a British prince, and the down-at-heel hamlet was transformed from an ugly duckling to an elegant swan.

Brighthelmston, as it was then known, only came to prominence in 1750 after local doctor Richard Russell publicised the health-giving properties of bathing in sea water and breathing in sea air, laying the foundations for its future as a spa town. A trickle of visitors became a flood after the place was patronised by the future George IV (1762–1830). It's not certain that fresh air and exercise cured him of enlarged glands following his first visit in 1783. However, the monument to his affection for the place – officially called Brighton after 1853 – remains the exotic, eccentric and illustrious Royal Pavilion.

Once a smart farmhouse, it was finally re-fashioned into its existing oriental-style grandeur by 1822 by John Nash (1752–1835), designer of London's Regent Street. Newly forged trade links with India were assuming mighty economic importance that was now to be reflected in architecture. The Pavilion's onion domes and sumptuous interiors revealed George's infamous indulgence and 'have-it-all' attitude that carried him into fearful debt. For this reason plans for richly appointed gardens were never carried out.

George fell in love with Maria Fitzherbert and she also took a house in Brighton. But her faith put paid to official marriage plans as by law the heir to the throne was not permitted a Catholic wife. They wed in secret and years later were still close. Under duress he eventually married a cousin, Caroline of Brunswick, a malodorous woman with a reputedly large sexual appetite. They honeymooned in Brighton and she bore him a daughter, Princess Charlotte. But in truth he so loathed her she was barred from his coronation. When he became king he persuaded Parliament to pass a law so that the marriage was 'for ever wholly dissolved, annulled and made void'.

An alcoholic, a gambler and a womaniser, George found plenty of amusements among the dubious entertainment that accompanied the growth of Brighton, including drinking houses, cock fighting and low-brow theatre. It's said that beneath the Pavilion there were at least two tunnels, one leading to the King's Arms, a favourite watering hole and brothel, and one to his stables so that he could avoid public derision after his popularity and looks faded.

The Pavilion was his proud legacy to Brighton. However, Queen Victoria was less enamoured and in 1850 she sold it to Brighton's municipal authority for a fraction of its cost.

In World War I it became a military hospital, with operations carried out on the giant kitchen tables. Plans to demolish it that were drawn up in the Thirties were resisted, an outcome that might have come back to haunt the people of Brighton after Nazi radio announcer Lord Haw Haw announced that the Pavilion would not be bombed as it was to be Hitler's home after he invaded Britain.

Opposite: *Despite echoes of Indian architecture, the Royal Pavilion is a testament to an English king's self-indulgent extravagance.*

FUN PALACES

Brighton prospered at the king's expense. His folly cost him dearly, but brought a fun palace feel to the town that it has never shaken off.

In 1823 a pier was built and delightful Regency-style houses with wedding cake edifices were cropping up all over the town. The arrival of the railway in 1841 brought many more trippers. As the service got quicker and cheaper so increasing numbers of Londoners visited, expanding the economy still further.

A second pier followed in 1863, the work of Victorian architect Eugenius Birch (1816–1884). Although he was responsible for 14 English seaside piers, including Blackpool's North Pier, this was deemed to be his finest. Within 20 years West Pier was graced with a magnificent theatre at its end.

After storm damage the original Regency pier was derelict, but there were grand designs for a replacement that cost £137,000 and took ten years to complete. When it opened in 1901 Brighton Marine Palace and Pier was now a centrepiece to the resort and offered plenty to the influx of visitors. However, it was bad news for Brighton indeed when piers went out of style, not least for the huge sums they cost in maintenance.

Despite its history, West Pier fell into disuse and was left a skeleton by a fire probably started by arsonists in 2003. Plans to re-fashion it are in the pipeline.

As for Brighton Marine Palace and Pier, it recovered from extensive damage caused by a barge adrift in heavy seas in 1975. Still, its once-glorious pavilion, removed in pieces to stop its collapse, has been replaced by an amusement arcade.

There were other venues for leisure seekers in Brighton during the 20th century. The town boasted no fewer than 17 cinemas between 1937 until the outbreak of World War II.

The oldest was the Duke of York's, built on the site of the Amber Ale Brewery in 1910 and decked with Edwardian finery. Inside there were 800 tip-up seats, an electric projector and luxurious Wilton carpets.

The Astoria, opened in 1933, contained 2,000 seats, while the cavernous Savoy accommodated no fewer than 2,300 when it opened its doors in 1930. Built on a former bathhouse, it soon became better known as the Canon.

Like piers, though, cinemas were old news by the 1950s and several were pulled down for new developments. That was the fate of the Hippodrome, an 1897 ice rink turned into a circus then a theatre, under the guidance of peerless designer Frank Matcham.

Several superstars headed the bill there including local comedian Max Miller, silent star Buster Keaton and singer Judy Garland. It even hosted The Beatles and The Rolling Stones before ending its era of live performances in 1965. However, there are plans to bring shows back to the Hippodrome so a new generation can cast their eyes over the exquisite décor that shouts aloud about the golden age of Edwardian England.

Below: *Brighton's pier, considered one of the most majestic ever constructed, reflects the refined nature of this south coast city.*

BRIGHTON ROCKS

For fifty years Brighton has been a Mecca for youth pursuing the elusive icon of chic. Famously it all began with a beach bust up in the spring of 1964 between mods and rockers.

The incident became a benchmark in adolescent rebellion yet the violence was far from extreme. It was more about young people re-defining the boundaries imposed by authority figures from radically different backgrounds.

Mods were sharp-suited young men in button-down Ben Sherman shirts, braces, commando boots and Parka coats. Typically they drove Vespa or Lambretta motorcycles – the more mirrors the better – and listened to Tamla Motown, ska or soul on the jukebox of their favourite Brighton coffee bar, The Zodiac. Musically they were corralled together with fans of The Who but many mods – short for modernists – have since denied this band was enormously significant.

Meanwhile rockers wore leather jackets and drove large motorbikes at great speed. Their anthems included hits by Eddie Cochrane and Buddy Holly. For no pressing reason, the groups victimised one another and chose to do so on a hitherto unknown scale on that infamous Whitsun holiday.

Some arrived already armed, others grabbed deckchairs for weapons, while more still resorted to stones from the beach. Police attempts to disperse more than 2,000 did little more than herd them to new fighting fields. The skirmish was sporadic but continued for the entire weekend.

At the end of the holiday, visitors were compelled to return home and Brighton was left bruised but unbowed.

It was not the only south coast resort targeted for trouble, but it became notorious for it through the film *Quadrophenia* in 1979. Of the 26 arrested – dubbed 'sawdust Caesars' in court – only five were local.

Predictions that this would be the norm for Brighton thereafter were wide of the mark as mods became victims of their passion for fashion. Followers grew tired of junking expensive clothes soon after purchase and sought new, less competitive outlets. The age of the hippie was just around the corner.

Still, young people were drawn to Brighton, not least by the University of Sussex, opened in 1961, and Brighton Polytechnic, established in 1968 and elevated to university status in 1992.

A former Brighton student, Norman Cook, returned to the town after success as a DJ and recording artist. A beach rave he planned in 2002 ended in disarray when 250,000 people descended on the town, clogging streets and the railway station. One reveller died after falling from some railings. Four years later Cook repeated the party, which this time was open only to those with a Brighton postcode.

Cook is a fan of Brighton and Hove Albion, the local football club, along with Des Lynam. It's had a chequered history, pinging up and down the league tables since its formation in 1901. Lowest spot in its fortunes came in 1995 when the home ground in Goldstone Road was sold. Now plans for a new stadium in Brighton are advancing, to the relief of 'Seagulls' fans everywhere. In 2000 the newly united boroughs of Brighton and Hove were awarded city status by Queen Elizabeth II.

Opposite: *Rebellious factions find a place for parades and parties in Brighton.*
Below: *Its close association with youth culture of various shades has helped the local economy to boom.*

THE SECRET WAR, SOUTH HEIGHTON

As the fortunes of war swung towards Nazi Germany in 1940, the people of Newhaven were suddenly thrust into the front line. Invasion appeared imminent and prospects were bleak.

After the Battle of Britain counterbalanced the fall of France those same residents of this sleepy South Downs town were once again at the cutting edge of the conflict. This time, though, they knew much less about it.

Beneath the chalk hills at the back of Newhaven there was a labyrinth of tunnels from which war action in the English Channel was orchestrated. Unseen by locals, the 20 m (60 ft) deep bunkers were a hive of activity involving up to 10,000 mostly forces staff. Known as HMS *Forward*, this 'stone frigate' was linked to radar that monitored everything under, on and above the English Channel between Dungeness and Selsey Bill.

To the untutored eye, though, there was no evidence of a vital Royal Naval Headquarters. Its entrance was down 122 steps from a hatch in room 16 of a country home in the village of South Heighton. Until the war it had provided holiday accommodation for city-bound staff of the Guinness Trust.

All the above-ground observation points were well hidden. One was a chicken shed with nest boxes disguising the gun emplacements. Beneath the ground there were two parallel tunnels extending some 63 m (190 ft) connected by five galleries. They housed the most advanced telephone and wireless technology of the era. Looking more like a colliery than a communications base, it nevertheless played a key role in the hunting of the German battleships *Scharnhorst* and *Prinz Eugen* in 1942, in the abortive Dieppe raid later the same year, and during the D-day landings of June 1944. That was in addition to co-ordinating air-sea rescues and spying on occupied France.

The acrid air within buzzed to the sound of Morse code. Women who answered the nationally-made plea to 'release a sailor for active service' often found themselves here after a spell of training, rapidly tapping out dot-dot-dash messages to commanders in the field. Ironically, while Newhaven residents were oblivious of its presence the more distant Germans were able to listen in if they successfully cracked the coded messages. The premises were shared with the Canadian Corps Coastal Artillery.

At the end of the war the complex was closed and largely forgotten. Except for the work of one man it might have stayed that way. However, Geoffrey Ellis was a schoolboy when the Royal Engineers turned up to build the tunnels,, and never forgot the quivering excitement of seeing the secret project get underway. Years later he researched the site and has done much to keep its memory alive.

He says: 'Initially, WRNS personnel staffed the W/T office, the teleprinters, the cipher office and the Naval Plot on a continuous three watch rota. They were supplemented by RN ratings for 'special' occasions and on D Day were joined by members of the RAF, WAAF and ATS. These crew wore headphones, not helmets; brandished morse keys rather than machine guns; dispatched bulletins, not bullets; and contemplated clandestine convoys in disciplined silence.'

Unknown heroes whose war stories were never heard, they nonetheless helped to speed the conflict to its end.

Opposite: *Newhaven beach became a front line in World War II after the fall of France.*

THE LIGHTHOUSES OF BEACHY HEAD

A treacherous coastline that's greedy for human life, the section of the
Sussex coastline edged by cliffs became known as a mariners' graveyard.

The number of bodies that washed up the south coast beaches so disturbed local parson Jonathan Derby (1667–1726) that he brandished pick and axe to enlarge a shoreline cave where he subsequently hung warning lanterns. But after his death the cave reverted to smugglers, and ships were once again at risk.

When merchant ship *The Thames* was beached in 1822 the subsequent loss of life touched a nerve with John Fuller (1757–1834). A famous philanthropist known variously as 'Honest John' and 'Mad Jack', he not only supplied Eastbourne with its first lifeboat but also financed a wooden lighthouse on the top of Beachy Head, known as Belle Tout for the ancient mound nearby.

By 1829 construction of a more substantial lighthouse began, with Sussex oxen used to drag giant blocks of Aberdeen granite to the site. When it opened on 11 October 1834 the lighthouse threw out beams equivalent to 22,000 candles that could be seen 37 km (23 miles) out at sea. It undoubtedly saved numerous lives – unless the weather was foggy when the light was cloaked. By 1895 it was resolved to build another lighthouse at Beachy Head, this time on the shoreline to offer maximum coverage for seamen.

The 43 metre (130 ft) candy-cane lighthouse was opened in 1902, home to three lighthouse keepers who arrived in a pulley-operated basket until it was fully automated in 1983.

This left the Belle Tout light redundant until neurologist Sir James Purves-Stewart bought it as a home. He built a road and extension, and installed an electric generator. His work received royal approval when King George VI and Queen Mary visited in 1935. However, when war broke out in 1939 the family were evacuated, and despite 30 cm (6 in) walls, their home was damaged in firing practice carried out on the Downs by the Canadian army.

Afterwards Purves-Stewart was compensated and the lighthouse was lovingly restored by other residents. But nature threatened to finish what World War II had started with wholesale erosion to the cliffs on which the lighthouse stood. Perched 95 m (285 ft) above the sea, subsequent owners watched in horror as the cliff edge moved ever closer with a series of landslips.

In 1999 Mark and Louise Roberts saw 6 m (20 ft) of their front garden descend into the sea and knew urgent action was needed. Aided by some talented engineers they hoisted their home onto greased runners and hauled it inland some 50 m (150 ft) in a painstaking operation

that, bizarrely, was complicated by the discovery of an unexploded bomb on the beach below.

It was a tense, expensive operation and initially the lighthouse travelled just 60 cm (2 ft) in three hours. Movers shovelled the chalky soil from around the foundations into wheelbarrows rather than risk another cliff fall by using mechanical machinery. It was set down with the likelihood of a further move 'up country' in mind.

Beachy Head is also known as a suicide spot and that's why it is patrolled for 100 hours a week by members of a chaplaincy team charged with talking people away from a point of no return.

Above left: *On the cliff the lighthouse is a charming anachronism.*
Above right: *At the sea edge it remains a life-saver in the English Channel, dubbed the busiest sea lane in the world.*

STARTLING SISTERS

Meandering into the distance the Seven Sisters cliffs are folding flashes of bright white that sever the connection between a blue sky and a deep blue sea. On a clear day the chalky glare stings the eyes.

Stretching between Seaford and Eastbourne each of the undulations has a name, although none is particularly romantic. The highest, Haven Brow, is followed by the curves of Short Brow and Rough Brow, Brass Point, Flat Hill, Bailey's Hill and Went Hill.

Tourists are seeing less of the cliffs each year, although the loss is impossible to discern with the naked eye. Erosion by weather and sea account for a 30–40 cm (12–14 in) annual retreat. Major collapses occur at individual locations perhaps once a decade. The sea wears away the soft chalk of the lower cliff until the unsupported weight of the top rocks carry them down. But once at the foot of the cliff these newly severed rocks act as sea defences, slowing the natural process for a while.

And among the fragments that descend to earth there's a wealth of fossils, harking back to when the Seven Sisters were made. It's thought the landscape dates back 700 to 100 million years when the bodies of countless thousands of small marine animals were pressed and preserved in the chalk layers. Scores of fossil hunters take to the shoreline in clement weather, confident of discovering a marker of the distant past. One of the most common finds is of an echinoid, the ancestor of the sea urchin that can still be found alive off the coast today.

There are also fascinating rock pools with live rather than long-dead contents including crabs, barnacles and limpets. Traces of the ships that have foundered here over the years – and there have been many – have been largely dispersed in the sea. It's one of the few stretches of coastline in the south to resist development, bar the occasional coastguard's cottage. The Seven Sisters are the South Downs, echo of Dover's White Cliff, on the North Downs. Film-makers have long realised that shots of the two sets of cliffs are interchangeable. For many they seem like a natural buttress when invaders from Europe have threatened.

But if the effects of erosion among the rolling cliffs offer no immediate cause for concern it's a different story at Birling Gap, a hamlet marking the end of the Seven Sisters. Already fishermen's cottages built in 1878 have been lost to the sea as the narrow cleft of land on which the village stands is undermined.

Relief then for the descendants of Carew Davies-Gilbert who was preparing to invest a sizeable chunk of his fortune in transforming the place with a building programme, a railway and a pier. His 1885 plans were ditched followed opposition from local landowners.

Some people are keen that unobtrusive sea defences are installed to secure the future of the small village. Mindful that the English Channel is likely to rise by as much as 54 cm (21 in) by 2080 as a result of climate change, others believe the coastline should be sacrificed to nature's forward march.

Opposite: *The verdant hills of the South Downs come to an abrupt end with white cliffs that daily face pummelling waves eager to free the fossils trapped within.*

LONDON

Presented by Meera Syal

Writer and comedienne, Meera Syal, celebrates the many faces of the capital city. With an iconic landmark on almost every corner, the city still showcases the work of Sir Norman Foster along the River Thames.

CITY/LANDMARKS/PALACES

Picture-postcard London has an icon on every corner. It celebrates the old while embracing the new, and pinpointing the panorama that captures its essence is an unenviable challenge.

Take the Gherkin, the building that replaced London's Baltic Exchange, blown up by the IRA in 1992. When plans for the pickle-shaped skyscraper were put on the table there were grumbles about its outrageous phallic symbolism. But before its completion in 2004 it had already won the hearts of Londoners and visitors alike – and bagged a hatful of awards. Properly called 30 St Mary Axe, it sits on a skyline clustered with other height-conscious constructions alongside many more ancient buildings that have all helped define the face of the city. For generations of ardent monarchists the place is all about royal palaces. There's Buckingham Palace, an existing town house transformed by the ambitions of George IV (1762–1830) and still the home of the Queen.

British hearts flutter when red-coated, shiny-stirruped soldiers march in perfect time towards it up the Mall in pleasingly ostentatious ritual.

It's not the only royal residence though. Among others there's Clarence House, the official home of Prince Charles and the Duchess of Cornwall, and Kensington Palace, built in 1605 when it lay in the then heart of the countryside, was the home of Princess Diana.

Across town, the Tower of London remains a royal palace although it's better known as the site of unspeakable acts and incarceration during the days of state-sanctioned torture and execution.

There are significant religious centres. Westminster Abbey, its cavernous interior busy with memorials to the

famous dead, has been thrust into the limelight following the immense success of *The Da Vinci Code*. A key part of the story is set there. Meanwhile the severe spires of numerous churches of forgotten London parishes reach up for air, no longer silhouetted as they once were thanks to new build.

Then there's Trafalgar Square, which plays host to England's number one annual New Year's Eve party. At its heart stands Nelson, the hero who fought the French and died in the process of winning the Battle of Trafalgar. Alas, arch enemy Napoleon was largely undeterred and continued rampaging across Europe for a further decade until the Battle of Waterloo put paid to his plans for world domination.

Despite standing on a 68 m (185 ft) platform Nelson is now dwarfed by buildings that have sprung up in the vicinity. Pigeons that once loved to perch – and worse – on his hat have been dispersed.

Piccadilly has been transformed from one of London's first shopping centres into traffic mayhem. Nonetheless the arcades maintain their charm as does the statue of Eros. These days shoppers are more likely to head for Regent Street and Oxford Street, where there's barely a passing place on the pavements.

London is bustling, buzzing, vibrant, pulsating, traditional and unorthodox – just as it was in the time of Dr Samuel Johnson (1709–1784). What he said about the city still holds good today:

'Sir, if you wish to have a just notion of the magnitude of this city, you must not be satisfied with seeing its great streets and squares, but must survey the innumerable little lanes and courts. It is not in the showy evolutions of buildings, but in the multiplicity of human habitations which are crowded together, that the wonderful immensity of London consists.'

Opposite: *Buckingham Palace, one of the homes of the British Royal family in London.*
Above left: *The once-terrible Tower of London.*
Above right: *Nelson atop his column – a well-loved London landmark.*

ST PAUL'S AND THE MILLENNIUM BRIDGE

As London suffocated in choking smoke after World War II bombs rained down, the comforting, clean curves of St Paul's Cathedral stood proud and unblemished. According to one observer: 'The dome seemed to ride the sea of fire.'

With a third of the city reduced to rubble, the stirring image grew to symbolise the stoutness and sturdy determination of both place and nation.

And if the war-time destruction then had any positive effect, it is that law forbids the building of skyscrapers and similar along the sightlines that lead to St Paul's so it still evokes a similar thrill to visitors wherever they choose to stand on the Thames' South Bank.

St Paul's Cathedral was built between 1675 and 1710 under the guidance of architect Sir Christopher Wren (1632–1723) after the Great Fire of London destroyed a previous model in 1666. Prophetically Christopher Wren announced: 'I build for eternity.' No fewer than four different monarchs reigned during its construction. Children are still thrilled by Wren's talents today as the

joys of the Whispering Gallery, and the extraordinary echoes it yields hold fast after more than 300 years. Its stunning interior was seen across the globe as it was the venue for the royal wedding between Prince Charles and Lady Diana Spencer in 1981.

The cathedral crypt contains the bodies of Nelson and the Duke of Wellington, the victor at Waterloo, as well as various articles that point up the site's medieval history, a reminder of the wealth of fascinating features that lay unseen beneath the streets linking it to the Middle Ages, Roman times and even to the prehistoric era.

There's no finer way to approach St Paul's than by the Millennium Bridge, a 325 m (975 ft) long pedestrian walkway spanning the Thames. Heralded as the first pedestrian river crossing for more than a century and a triumph in art and design, it was opened in 2000. As many as 100,000 people flocked to tread the broad aluminium deck. And then its problems began.

Children shrieked with delight, mothers furrowed anxious brows, and the less sure-footed clung to the sides as the bridge began to wobble. Some people disembarked from the oscillating path complaining of sea-sickness. Investigations revealed it was the way in which people were walking that caused the bridge to bobble. Within two days it was closed and red-faced engineers employed an army of bridgewalkers to discern why footfall was causing such difficulties in a facility expressly designed for pedestrians. By 2002 all the problems had been rectified and countless millions have used it, their view of London unimpeded by support wires that are channelled beneath.

Squaring up to St Paul's at the opposite end of the bridge is Tate Modern, the former Bankside power station closed in 1981 that's now the home to Britain's finest modern art collections. A seven-storey hallway which once housed electricity generators is now the venue of ambitious installations that are coupled as much with controversy as with acclaim.

Certainly Shakespeare would have been left scratching his head at some of the outlandish monuments constructed in the name of art. His rebuilt theatre, the Globe, is just a stone's throw away, overshadowed by the Tate Modern but possibly not outclassed.

Opposite: *The view of St Paul's from the South Bank is unhindered by new arrivals on the block, including the Millennium Bridge.*
Below: *The Tate Modern.*

CITY MARKETS

Underneath the arches of London Bridge station is the unlikely location of a gourmet's paradise. The aroma of exotic coffee mingles with that of fresh-cut flowers, there's handmade chocolate and cheese, patisserie and potatoes.

This is Borough Market, a foodie's fantasy flourishing in an age when the supermarket aspires to be king. It claims to be the oldest market in London, functioning since Roman times, and has occupied its present site for 250 years.

But perhaps it's not the age that's remarkable but the fact that it has survived at all. Once London was littered with such markets. The testament of this lies in street names such as Milk Yard, Leather Lane, Bread Street, Cloth Fair and Wool Road, denoting the goods sold there.

Painter and satirist William Hogarth (1697–1764) frequently made London's markets and fairs the backdrop of his work. While Gin Lane in his famous work depicting the perils of alcohol may well have been artistic licence, markets were a pivotal part of city life.

When the Thames was frozen, as happened on more than 20 occasions in the 17th and 18th centuries, the markets moved on to the ice in the form of a Frost Fair.

Commercial forces shaped by new shopping trends meant that street markets and basket sellers gave way to larger, specialist centres. Billingsgate was another long-standing market, in existence in the 11th century and possibly long before, which evolved as the centre of fish sales. The women who used to work there wore heavy

skirts and padded petticoats, while hair and cap became one with the stinking liquid that seeped from the fish-filled baskets they carried on their heads. These were tough, gin-drinking, pipe-smoking, eel-flinging types who knew foul language and weren't afraid to use it. We pay tribute to them today when we use the term 'fishwife', for this is where it was coined.

Another long-standing market was Smithfields, soon devoted to meat. In 1174 the site was described by William Fitzstephen, clerk to Thomas à Becket, as 'a smooth field where every Friday there is a celebrated rendezvous of fine horses to be sold, and in another quarter are placed vendibles of the peasant, swine with their deep flanks, and cows and oxen of immense bulk.' Those fine horses were apparently raced on a regular basis at Smithfields and there were sporting spectacles too, including wrestling and bear-baiting.

But its history goes beyond that of meat sales as it was associated with notorious executions. Scottish rebel William Wallace and Wat Tyler, head of the 14th century Peasant's Revolt, were hung, drawn and quartered here, while 43 Protestants were burnt to death at Smithfields during the reign of Queen Mary I (1553–1558). Evidence of the outrage was recently excavated at the site.

Covent Garden has had an Italianate face since the 1630s, and was for centuries the home of a fruit and vegetable market. Today's shoppers find themselves walking the paths trodden by Londoners for centuries. But while purchasing fashion has changed, the ambience of London life has stayed the same.

Above, left and right: *For centuries markets have been a significant feature of London life, providing necessities and luxuries in equal measure.*

CANARY WHARF

Anchoring the London skyline is a giant obelisk at Canary Wharf, the building that brought the capital's business community into the modern age. It marks the grave of London's docks and an against-all-odds resurgence of East London.

At a whopping 235 m (771 ft), One Canada Square is the capital's tallest building, shiny with nearly 4,000 windows and winking conspiratorially at Londoners 40 times every minute with the aircraft warning light atop its pyramid roof. More than 90,000 people work both here and in the new complexes that surround it, on land that is bound by a U-bend in the river.

Yet once – not long ago – before its foundations were conceived more than 100,000 people worked along the stretch of river lying east of Tower Bridge in and among the docks. Shipping was vital for an island nation and here goods were ferried straight into the centre of the capital.

From the Middle Ages, tonnage grew as did the number of operational wharves and warehouses. One was piled high with coffee beans while its neighbour was heavy with sugar. For several centuries it was as easy to get a pineapple in London's markets as it was in the tropics. In fact, it earned its name from trade links with the Canary Islands.

Pretty it wasn't, but the docklands were a thriving enterprise. Variously in history the area was also associated with brothels and opium dens, and was the original Chinatown. Before the start of World War II in excess of 35 million tons of cargo were hauled ashore here from countless thousands of ships. Even war-time bombing raids which flattened the area could not destroy its vibrant merchant trade. The docks were back in action in the Sixties dealing with more goods than ever before.

But air freight, archaic working practices and out-of-town competitors took their toll and by the 1980s the docks had died, robbing thousands of London families of jobs and prospects.

One edge of London was left barren and no one was quite sure what to do about it. The Corporation of the City of London had been fending off grand expansion plans by big business in an effort to preserve the antiquity of The Square Mile. Finally companies saw an opportunity to create the large, modern, open-plan offices that they craved just a stone's throw from London's existing commercial heart.

By 1989 London had turned its face away from the past towards a glittering future with a set of ambitious blueprints. The enormous tower at Canary Wharf was to be flanked by twins some 35 m (100 ft) shorter. There would be abundant office space, new shops, better transport links and excellent restaurants.

Unfortunately the enormous project coincided with a property crash that left not one, but two companies associated with its construction in difficulties. Finally the economic mood changed, as did the feelings of residents who were initially opposed to the plans. One Canada Square opened for rental in 1991 and subsequently the 39 ha (97 acre) site has been largely filled with facilities, except for the 8 ha (20 acres) of landscaped open spaces, that is.

It takes 40 seconds to ascend to the 50th floor at One Canada Square in the elevator. The area's dizzying rise to prominence has also taken a ludicrously short time, despite a shaky start.

Opposite: *Canary Wharf overshadows the surrounding buildings and impressively dominates the Docklands' skyline.*

LONDON EYE

Looming over London is the Eye, focused on the far distance. A fairground ferris wheel gone large, it hoists its capsule passengers 135 m (400 ft) into the air for an unhindered bird's-eye view of the capital.

The wheel slotted in an 'A' frame is dotted with 32 clear cabins, each representing one of the London boroughs. A magnificent feat of engineering, its symmetry is pleasing – and so, for the operators, are visitor numbers, with 3.5 million passengers notched up since its opening in 2000.

At its full height passengers aboard are standing taller than the top of St Paul's Cathedral but are beneath the satellite dishes on BT Tower. It was inspired by a ferris wheel that stood in Earl's Court more than a century ago. For the moment it is the tallest attraction of its type in the world but there are plans to haul a bigger wheel into place on the Las Vegas Strip standing at 170 m (510 ft), and another in Berlin at 185 m (555 ft).

A circuit on the wheel takes 30 minutes, during which time the vista expands to a distance of 40 km (25 miles) on a clear day, encompassing Windsor Castle, and all the views of London, north and south, then contracts once more as the capsule descends to earth. Throughout it is possible to trace the meandering River Thames, the grey-blue shiny path that dissects the capital.

And observant Eye travellers might spot modern Mudlarks at work, treasure-hunters armed with metal detectors scouring the river banks at low tide. Not only is

it a highly dangerous pastime thanks to the vagaries of the tide, but it also needs a permit. However, the finds made in the malodorous mud of a river once dubbed 'liquid history' are transforming our perception of medieval childhood with toy guns and figures as well as children's shoes from the era coming to light.

Today's treasure seekers take their name from the children that once haunted the river banks searching for coal, wood and bones to sell. In the 1840s, Victorian journalist Henry Mayhew wrote:

'...(Mudlarks) may be seen at daybreak, very often, with their trousers tucked up, groping about, and picking out the pieces of coal from the mud. They go into the river up to their knees, and in searching the mud they very often run pieces of glass and long nails into their feet. When this is the case, they go home and dress the wounds, and return directly, for, should the tide come up without their finding anything, they must starve that day.'

After the sewerage system herringboned through the city Mudlarks were joined by Toshers, looking for jewellery and money accidentally flushed away.

At the time the river was also known for its shocking stink and one can only imagine how many Mudlarks and Toshers succumbed to the diseases it bore. Finally the river became intolerable even for fish. But an enduring clean-up campaign has reversed the ill effects of industry and population. The waters of the Thames are now so clean that they are home to 115 species of fish, numerous birds, the occasional seal and even, on one memorable occasion in 2006, a bottlenose whale. It seems the 7-ton creature took a wrong turn into the North Sea and tried to return to its Atlantic feeding grounds by taking a 'short-cut' up the Thames. Sadly, he perished before he could be returned to deep water.

Above: *One of 21st century tourism's big hitters, the London Eye dwarfs its neighbours on the South Bank.*

WATERLOO SUNSET

Looking down on London tells you how the city has sprawled, where the river meanders and which attraction has the best edifice.

Then there's the ground-level perspective from streets shaking with the thunder of traffic on pavements swarming with people drawn from all over the globe. Only now can the sounds of the city vibrate your eardrum, can your eyes make sense of the spectacle.

The best spot to stand is a badly kept secret. A curve in the path of the river means that Waterloo Bridge offers the most advantageous angle to a section of riverfront where London's best bits jostle for attention.

Looking west there's the hard-edged façade of the Royal Festival Hall, a first-rate concert venue dating from the Festival of London in 1951. It is closely surrounded by the block concrete of other buildings in what's now known as the Southbank Centre, all constructed at the end of the 1960s and still receiving bouquets and brickbats in equal measure.

Beyond stands the London Eye, a dominant feature but still not sufficiently mighty to blot out the Houses of Parliament. In 1834 the previous parliament building burned down and six years later the foundation stone of today's building was laid. Flanked on one side by Big Ben, its in-vogue gothic elegance was the work of Sir Charles Barry (1795–1860). Much of the detail was provided by colleague Augustus Pugin who was just 24 when he undertook the project. Queen Victoria officially opened it in 1852.

Dragging your eyes down the river there's Cleopatra's Needle, a gift from Egypt following victory over Napoleon. However, the red granite obelisk – a genuine Ancient Egyptian artefact although not linked with Cleopatra – was left overseas smothered in the dust of the Alexandrian desert for decades by a government unwilling to finance relocation. Finally it was brought to England in 1878, in a fraught journey paid for by public subscription.

It was put up on top of a time capsule and flanked by two bronze sphinxes, which were reproductions made in Victorian England. This curious composition is completed by hieroglyphics added in the time of Moses alongside the names of sailors who died during the Needle's voyage to England. In 1917 an air raid by the Germans left one of the sphinxes with shrapnel damage, which it wore like a badge of courage until recently.

The Needle is supposed to be haunted by the ghost of a naked man. Many have seen him run from the obelisk and throw himself into the river but no one has yet heard a splash.

The scene is cut through by embankments each side of the river. Now they are much-loved illuminated promenades but their purpose when they were built in 1875 was to cover the newly installed sewers.

As for the bridge itself, it was built during World War II as a replacement for the first, which dated from 1817 when a keeper demanded a toll from users. The station nearby isn't original either. It was rebuilt in 1900 to improve on a predecessor, opened in 1848 when victory over Napoleon more than 30 years previously still tasted sweet.

Waterloo Bridge is sometimes associated with misery, not just among the thousands of commuters who use it each day, but by the death of Georgi Markov, the Bulgarian dissident who in 1978 was shot by a platinum pellet fired from a gun disguised as an umbrella. He died three days later from the effects of the deadly ricin that had been added to the pellet.

But there's a feel on the bridge, a 'love London' emotion that's wrapped up in the Kinks' song *Waterloo Sunset*. As its writer Ray Davies notes: 'As long as I gaze at Waterloo sunset, I am in paradise.'

Opposite: *Watch London's sunset from Waterloo Bridge to see the city at its most memorable.*
Right: *Is Cleopatra's Needle haunted by a naked man?*

BATH

Presented by

Sir Ranulph Fiennes

Britain's premier explorer marvels
at the city's architecture and
cultural heritage over the centuries
from Roman baths to Georgian
royal crescents.

LIQUID GOLD

After the Romans invaded England in 43 AD they discovered a way to turn water into gold. The alchemy held good for centuries and Bath is still cleaning up today.

There was little to distinguish Bath from anywhere else in Britain when the Romans first arrived more than two centuries ago, save a boggy field that held special significance for locals. To them it was a magical place, for the oozing mud was warm even when the weather was not. No one knew the site was atop an old volcano from which thermal springs gurgled forth freely. However, this was not an uncommon phenomenon for the widely travelled invaders.

Now the Romans set about doing what they did best. Capitalising on the engineering techniques honed at home in Rome they began building a baths for health and religious purposes. A temple devoted to Minerva – a Roman equivalent to the Greek god Athena and known as 'the goddess of a thousand works' – encased the sacred spring. Typically, the Romans had no interest in proselytising and acknowledged the locals' preference for a different deity by naming it Aquae Sulis, for the Celtic god that had been worshipped there previously.

The Roman-built pool was lined with 45 sheets of lead and had piping that took excess water off into the River Avon. It was such a popular place – and the weather was so unpredictable – that they eventually built a roof over the top some 40 m (120 ft) high, dimensions unseen outside London.

If the lavish building programme was not enough to leave the resident Celts in awe, then the calibre of visitor that made a pilgrimage there surely would be. The devout poured into the area from all over the Roman Empire, wealthy and sophisticated beyond measure.

But Roman expectations that the brand would go nationwide were frustrated. This is the only warm springs in Britain, exuding 1,170,000 litres (240,000 gallons) of water at a temperature of 46 degrees every day.

And Bath is one of the finest classical temples bequeathed to Britain by the Romans. The spiritual importance of Bath was underlined by the discovery of 12,000 Roman coins made as votive offerings. Excavations that took place 30 years ago also found a stash of Roman curses, appeals scratched on thin lead or pewter to the goddess to exact revenge on an enemy. They were directed against thieves, love rivals, business or even courtroom adversaries. Even if the pleas went unanswered there was undoubtedly a therapeutic effect.

'May he who has stolen Vilbia from me become as liquid as water...' read one, while another said: 'I curse him who has stolen my hooded cloak, whether man or woman, whether slave or free, that... the goddess Sulis inflict death upon... and not allow him sleep or children now and in the future...'

It's unlikely that there's any truth in the legend that Prince Bladud founded Bath a few centuries earlier than the Romans when he realised the soothing, bubbly mud cured him of leprosy. According to legend he was educated in Athens, founded Stamford University in Lincolnshire and became the ninth King of the Britons before plunging to his death, Icarus-style, in trying to fly with man-made feathered wings. Nonetheless, a statue depicting him stands by the baths.

Opposite: *Bath's popularity as a spa was established by invading Romans who were master bath builders.*

HIGH SOCIETY

Beau Nash was a man with a mission, to make Bath the finest and most fashionable venue of 18th century England. Despite powdered wig and be-jewelled buckle, he did so in considerable style.

Born in Swansea in 1674, Nash struggled to find his riche. Rather than a recognised career, he found life as a well dressed dandy rubbing shoulders with society's high fliers much more to his liking.

When Nash arrived in Bath in 1705 it was in the wake of a visit by Queen Anne (1665–1714) that had focussed a spotlight on the city. Realising its potential, he embarked on a benevolent dictatorship that shaped that city for decades.

He then began to make his mark as Master of Ceremonies, the official charged with organising the city's social calendar. With plenty of experience of London's social scene already behind him he understood just what was required and set about structuring a disciplined social system to safeguard polite society. First, though, he raised money to repair Bath's dilapidated roads and then

upgraded the quality of lodgings. He insisted on renovations and then, after inspection, personally set a tariff for every room available.

In 1708 he commissioned Bath Assembly House, paid for by subscriptions raised from Bath's visitors. To ensure the venue had no rivals he forbade private parties, and thereafter all concerts, balls and teas were held there.

At first a rule breaker – he dipped out of Oxford University, the army and the law – Beau Nash became a prolific rule maker.

Some of his regulations were admirable. He forbade the wearing of swords after his predecessor's untimely death in a duel following a card game. The fashion for thigh-length boots among men gave way to more sensible stockings and shoes at his instigation. Also, he curbed hard drinking, swearing, smoking and late nights, decreeing that balls should begin at six in the evening and end at eleven, to maximise the health benefits of the waters.

His other rules included 'that all repeaters of such lies and scandal be shunned by all company – except such as have been guilty of the same crime.' Brutally honest, he was anxious that people knew their place so 'elder ladies and children be contented with a second bench at the ball as being past or not come to perfection.'

Perhaps his biggest social triumph was in bridging the huge chasm that had previously existed between the aristocracy and the rapidly expanding ranks of the middle classes. This ultimately meant that the social spectrum in Bath was broad, rather than hamstrung by outdated convention.

At his invitation famous figures from England's social scene stayed in Bath, and even lauded socialites from Europe made the journey. An inveterate gambler himself, he urged caution among those who were less *au fait* with the hazards of the gaming table, and was charitable to those less fortunate.

But it was gambling that would be his undoing. A change in the betting laws hit his income that was mostly derived from gambling. And like every fashion icon, he eventually went out of vogue. Having sold most of his possessions, he lived in straightened circumstances until his death in 1762. But his legacy was a buzzing, thriving, buoyant Bath.

Opposite: *The Assembly Rooms, Bath.*
Below left: *Stamping his mark on Bath, dapper dandy Beau Nash made it the hub of English polite society.*
Below right: *Popjoys Restaurant at Beau Nash House.*

BATH STONE

The distinctive honey hues common to Bath's buildings are from stones whose history outstrips the city by a considerable margin.

They were formed when the region was under a shallow sea some 170 million years ago as sediment coated with lime was laid in seams of various depths close to the River Avon. Bath stone is a type of freestone, that is, one that can be cut or squared in any direction. However, it has to be set in the building in the same way that it came out of the ground, so there is a distinct 'right' and a 'wrong' way to stack blocks after they have been extracted.

The Romans began mining it to build the baths, but they did well to recognise its potential as at first sight it does not seem fit for the purpose. As one observer noted in 1754: 'There is no stone that differs so much in its bed, after it has been wrought and exposed to the air as the Bath freestone. While it is in the ground, it is soft, moist, yellowish, and almost crumbly and it seems very little more than congealed sand and that not well concreted together. But when it has been some time exposed to the air and is thoroughly dried, it becomes white, hard, firm and an excellent stone.'

Bath stone has been exported across Britain and the world and features in Truro Cathedral, Cornwall, Nuneaton Grammar School in the Midlands, Gloucester Guildhall, Cape Town town hall, and Union Station in Washington.

Locally it has done much to lend a uniform identity to the city. In the Georgian era it was boom time for nearby mines. One man who got in at the ground floor was Ralph Allen (1693–1764), Bath's post master who became prominent after he devised a cash-saving method of horse-back letter delivery with routes that by-passed London. He used some of the fortune he had accrued to buy workings at Combe Down and Bathampton Down in 1726, just as the development of Bath was gaining momentum.

Miners removed the stone using chisels and bars. It wasn't until halfway through the following century that labour-saving long saws were introduced. However, ahead of his time, Allen installed a tram system that transported wagons from mines or quarries at speed to the River Avon, where it was needed for distribution.

To advertise the attractive qualities of the stone Allen had his own Palladian house, Prior Park, perched above Bath, constructed in it. In 1742, shortly afterwards, he became mayor of Bath and between 1757 and 1764 was the city's Member of Parliament.

Allen's investment in Bath stone made him wealthier still. However, he used the money wisely, building accommodation for miners among other worthy projects. He donated £1,000 and all the stone needed to build the city hospital. One of his partners in the venture was Dr William Oliver (1695–1764), creator of the Bath Bun and the Bath Oliver biscuit, both originally intended to abet the health of his patients.

Mellow stone quarried from the hills surrounding Bath has been used locally – such as for the Guildhall (opposite)*, the Roman Baths and Grand Abbey* (below left) *and the Palladian bridge* (below right) *– and also exported worldwide.*

NOVEL LOATHING

In an age when anyone with aspirations in England was beating a path to Bath, novelist Jane Austen (1775–18) yearned to escape its elegant clutches. While others looked upon fine buildings in soft stone with pleasure, her hazel eyes surveyed them with disdain.

On her approach to Bath for the first time she saw it was 'all vapour, shadow, smoke and confusion.' Later she wrote dismissively to sister Cassandra: 'Bath is still Bath.'

She continued to voice her weariness in *Northanger Abbey* with the line: 'Do you know, I get so immoderately sick of Bath.'

Quite where the shortfall lay nobody is sure as Bath was, and remains, one of the most stunning cities in Britain. Austen was born the seventh of eight children in a village near Basingstoke in Hampshire and there's no doubt she and her family were blissfully happy there. But in 1801 her father the Reverend George Austen gave up his church and retired to Bath, a place previously visited by the family on at least two occasions.

Jane enjoyed dancing – and Bath with its population of 35,000 had its fair share of balls. Her complaint seems to have been that events in Bath were too small and sedate for her enjoyment. Shopping was another favourite pastime and in Bath there was Milsom Street, still a shopper's delight, and the outlets recently opened on Pulteney Bridge. Not an urban animal, the possibilities did not move her. If she hoped to find a suitable man – the avowed aim of many of her fictional heroines – then she was to be disappointed. She remained unwed until her death.

What baffles most is that in letters written throughout her stay in Bath she fails to comment on the architectural glories that draw paragraphs of praise from today's visitors. It could be that letters in which she waxed lyrical about the attractions of Bath have yet to come to light, the few in existence from the five-year spell she spent in the city skewing her message to subsequent generations. In total only 160 letters penned by Jane during her lifetime have survived as many were destroyed by her loyal sister after her death.

Still Jane featured Bath in two novels, *Northanger Abbey*, completed in 1803 while she lived there, and *Persuasion* in 1817. In Austen terms Bath provides the gritty realism of Regency England, not so much in the place as the people. Among a population drawn to the recently wrought city she found oppressive courtesy, artificial emotions, snobbery and rampant self-interest. This was rich cloth for the satires that she so expertly crafted. There's no doubt she was more at home in rural Hampshire, where she returned after her time in Bath and resumed a writing career armed with plenty of material for the ironic and witty insights for which she is now famous. She died aged 41 in Winchester after apparently suffering from Addison's Disease, a rare endocrine disorder at the time unidentified.

Bath is untarnished by Austen's misgivings. It has chosen to cash in on its Austen connections and fans across the world make their way here to luxuriate in her oblique social commentary that even today seems in keeping amid Bath's grand style.

Opposite: *An early 19th-century illustration for Austen's* Northanger Abbey, *which she set in Bath despite her own disdain for the city.*

PALLADIAN PRIDE

'Then Bath spread herself before us, like a beautiful dowager giving a reception. Bath, like Edinburgh, has the rare trick of surprising you all over again. You know very well it is like that, yet somehow your memory must have diminished the wonder of it, for there it is, taking your breath away again.'

Journalist and activist J. B. Priestly (1894–1984) speaks for most when he recalls the thrill of seeing Bath after a long absence or for the first time.

Its effect is due in no small part to a 16th century Italian who tore up the rule book about architecture and wrote another that prevailed for centuries.

Andrea di Pietro della Gondola (1508–1580) was born in Padua, part of the previously powerful Venetian republic. Travels around Italy helped him define the Palladian style for which he is known. Under his professional name, Palladio, he summed up his principles of design in *The Four Books of Architecture*, a bible to later generations of builders.

When Bath was being built it was to these guidelines that draughtsmen referred, including Robert Adam (1728–1792). During his 'grand tour' around Europe in 1754 he absorbed the Palladian influences he found there like a sponge.

Asked to build a bridge spanning the Avon 15 years later, Adam had no doubts which way to turn. Adam revived and modified a plan by Palladio for the Ponte di Rialto in Venice that was ultimately thrown out – proof that even geniuses are sometimes knocked back.

The result was Pulteney Bridge, completed in 1773 and enabling the previously isolated Bathwick to become a city suburb. It was built at the request of William and Frances Pulteney who wished to capitalise on land they had inherited on the far bank of the Avon river.

Pulteney Bridge is one of only four bridges in the world to incorporate shops in its design, the most famous being Ponte Vecchio in Florence. The initial splendour of Bath's romantic new bridge was shortlived, however, as floods in 1799 and 1800 caused extensive damage. Ad hoc modifications carried out since have altered its appearance. Now only one aspect, best seen from Parade Gardens, gives due credit to Adam's innovation. This marks the end of the navigable stretch of river – it's backed by a weir – and is close to the river's junction with the Kennet and Avon canal.

Palladian architecture usually boasts a prominent column-bearing feature flanked by complementary wings on either side. Its characteristics have helped win Bath the accolade of being a UNESCO World Heritage Site.

The springs remain an important feature, too. After water-borne bugs were discovered in 1978 the spring water was no longer open to bathers. An ambitious plan to build a public spa echoing Bath's Roman history was formulated. The building's design by Sir Nicholas Grimshaw owed nothing to Palladian style, having been nick-named 'the glass cube'. And when it finally opened in 2006 the spa was millions of pounds over budget. Still, it's another draw to a city that has been burdened in the 21st century by falling visitor numbers.

Opposite: *Pulteney Bridge not only spans the river but is also a shopping venue, lending Bath a European feel.*

CIRCUS AND CRESCENT, TWO MARKS OF DISTINCTION

Two sites sum up all that is best about Bath. Extraordinary even by today's technology, the gracious curves of the Circus and the Royal Crescent recall the heyday of Georgian England and were built thanks to one family's talents.

The son of a builder, John Wood the Elder (1704–1754) experimented with designs in London's Oxford Street before turning his attentions to Bath. Once there he developed a powerful vision to put Bath on a par with ancient Rome.

First came Queen's Square in 1728, followed by North and South Parades, characterised by a theme of quiet dignity running through the developments. The blueprints for Bath Assembly Rooms followed – but he saved the best until last.

The Circus was housing-in-the-round in three lofty and elliptical equal sections, dissected by roadways. From above the effect is of a circle punctured by the points of a triangle. To some it summons up images of the Coliseum in Rome where gladiators fought and Christians perished. In fact it is more reminiscent of Stonehenge. Wood borrowed the prehistoric monument's measurements laid down years before in the creation of the Circus. Also, he incorporated acorn finials, reminiscent of the legend of Bladud rather than the Romans who did so much to fashion the city as if to define the cultural differences. The appearance of Masonic symbols among 525 emblems on a frieze that runs around the top prompted suspicions that Wood had strong links with the esoteric group that was beginning to make headway in England in the first half of the 18th century.

He laid the foundation stone just weeks before his death. Now it was down to John Wood the Younger (1728–1782) to deliver on his father's masterpiece. Sited just outside the walls of the medieval city, the development swallowed up land. Hampered by an economic blip, there was a delay while Wood purchased the necessary plots. Nevertheless, the first houses were completed in 1755 and the final work carried out by 1766. Judging by their present ample girth the London plane trees in the centre of the Circus were planted at about that time.

Among the most famous of Circus tenants was artist Thomas Gainsborough (1727–1788) whose career as a portrait painter sky-rocketed after moving to Bath.

Hardly breaking stride, Wood quickly moved on to his next project – the Royal Crescent. This was half-moon housing, bare and rhythmic in design, that was finished by 1775.

Some of Royal Crescent's residents have been famous, including Frederick, Duke of York, son of King George III and the inspiration for the children's nursery rhyme *The Grand Old Duke of York*.

Some residents were short-lived. Vicomte Jean Baptiste du Barre came to Bath in the summer of 1778 with his wife and sister, and one Captain Rice, an Irish Jacobite. They leased No. 8 Royal Crescent, hosting lavish card parties to profit from the gambling mania that gripped the city. One night they quarrelled over £600 winnings from another Royal Crescent resident. Rice threw down his glove and a duel was arranged at Claverton Down. Du Barre fired first, and wounded his friend in the thigh. But Rice's aim was more deadly: the Frenchman was hit in the chest and died within moments.

The Circus (opposite) *and Royal Crescent* (below) *are internationally known landmarks that have distinguished Bath from other cities since the 18th century.*

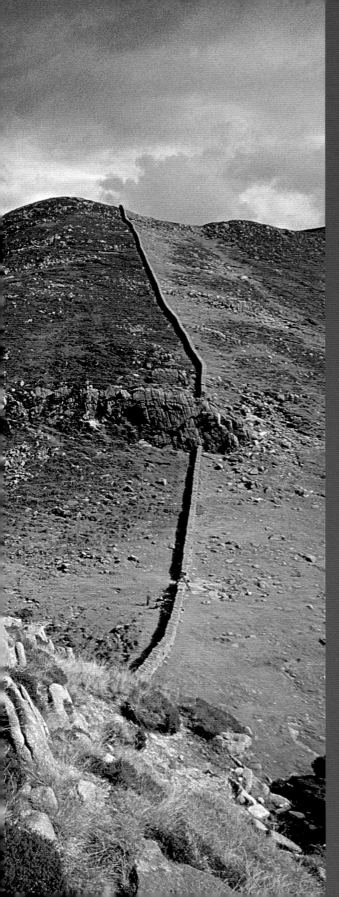

CO. DOWN

Presented by Eddie Irvine

Racing icon Eddie Irvine takes time
out to rediscover the beauty of this
magical kingdom of County Down,
Strangford Lough, the reborn city
of Belfast, and of course the
Mountains of Mourne.

ST PATRICK'S MISSION

It seems like every corner of Co. Down has some link with Ireland's patron saint, St Patrick. Beneath fictional accounts of snake-banishings and slaughtered monsters there's a fascinating glimpse of his evangelical mission – an insight into Northern Ireland's importance as a cradle of Christian theology.

For someone whose name symbolises Irish pride worldwide – and St Patrick's March 17th feast day has now become a huge global céilidh – it's surprising how few hard facts are known about the saint's life. From his own scant writings we can deduce that he was born into a wealthy British family around 400 AD, was captured by Irish slave traders in his mid-teens and forced to work as a shepherd, possibly on Slemish Mountain, Co. Antrim.

After six years an angel called Victoricus apparently appeared to him in a dream and urged him to escape. He is said to have walked 320 km (200 miles) before catching a boat back to Britain where he entered the priesthood and was ordained a bishop within a decade. Victoricus then returned carrying letters, one of which 'The Voice of the Irish' pleaded with him to lead a mission to Ireland. Sometime around 432 AD, Patrick is said to have landed on the banks of the River Slaney near Strangford Loch and begun the task of converting heathens.

It is perhaps no coincidence that the previous year Pope Celestine had sent his envoy Palladius as 'the first bishop to the Irish believing in Christ'. It's unclear what happened to Palladius and almost nothing is known of his time in Ireland. One obvious possibility is that he was rather too up-front for the tastes of pagan leaders and his conversion of the masses away from the 'old religion' may have been an unpopular, even fatal, strategy. That said, life in Ireland would have been hard and unforgiving, a world away from Rome's civilising influence, and it's equally likely that Palladius died of natural causes.

Either way, St Patrick's knowledge of Irish ways ensured he was well equipped for his mission. His first conversion was an influential local warlord, Dichu, brother of Ulster's High King, and he delivered his first sermon at Saul, Co. Down, in a barn donated by Dichu (a replica of an early church and round tower now stands on the site). With the nobility on side it was easier to convince commoners and Patrick proved a master at adapting pagan images to his cause.

He is said to have used the three leaves of the shamrock to explain the Holy Trinity and is credited with incorporating the sun – a powerful heathen god – into drawings of the cross. There are also plainly ludicrous claims about his power, such as the suggestion that he drove all snakes out of Ireland (there never were any in the first place) and killed a lake monster. These are almost certainly folk memories in which the creatures symbolised pagan beliefs.

Patrick made sure he stamped Christianity's mark on 'nature worship' and four springs set in a secluded valley at Struell Wells, Co. Down, were in obvious need of early blessing. This place was once a pagan religious shrine but following Patrick's prayers it attracted pilgrims from across Europe, all anxious to bathe in waters rumoured to have healing properties. Curiously, a shadow of paganism lingered here for centuries; as late as 1774 there were reports of vast gatherings for the two great festivals of Midsummer's Eve and Lammas.

The date of St Patrick's death, and the site of his grave, are as intangible as much of his life. Some historians claim his remains lie at Glastonbury, in the west of England, although the Irish will always take some convincing. Current received wisdom is that he died at Raholp, near Saul, in 461 AD, and was given the last rites by his friend St Tassach. His gravestone can be seen in Downpatrick, near Down Cathedral.

Left: *A stone slab marks the reputed burial place of St Patrick in Downpatrick Cathedral, Co. Down.*

CRADLE OF KNOWLEDGE

You might think the thriving seaside resort of Bangor, Co. Down, would sit awkwardly alongside the great Christian spiritual centres of Rome, Lourdes and Canterbury. You'd be wrong. By the 7th century AD Bangor Abbey was a major player in Church affairs, so much so that it appears on the world's most important medieval map – the Mappa Mundi.

According to monastic chronicles collectively known as the Irish Annals, the abbey was founded on the southern edge of Belfast Lough sometime around 552 AD by St Comgall. The area was known locally as the 'Vale of Angels' because St Patrick had once rested there and seen the valley filled with them. Rarely, it seems, was there a dull day in Patrick's life.

Comgall, who served as a soldier, had followed a particularly severe lifestyle on his island retreat in Lough Erne – one long round of prayers, penances, vigils and fasting. He'd intended to set up monasteries in Britain but was eventually dissuaded from this by his bishop, Lugidius, who convinced him that Ireland had greater need of his talents.

Comgall took his principles with him to Bangor and, despite the strict regime, quickly established a large community eager to benefit from his knowledge. Apart from the scriptures, monks studied mathematics, geometry, logic and music, learnt Latin verse, and honed their talents as artists. As pupils grew in confidence they were sent out to found new monasteries elsewhere, and by the time of St Comgall's death around 602 AD – sources differ on the date – more than 3,000 monks across Ireland looked to the Abbot of Bangor as their guide and mentor. In terms of importance it was second only to Armagh.

Evidence for this can be seen in a 1,400-year-old document called the *Antiphonary of Bangor*; a collection of Latin hymns, prayers and antiphons (verses sung by two separate groups of monks) which is regarded by historians as a priceless witness to early European monastic life. It reveals an extraordinary standard of artwork and literacy – but sadly for the Irish was removed 1000 years ago to Bobbio in Italy, where it is still housed.

Another reference to Bangor Abbey appears in an 8th-century copy of St Matthew's Gospel, produced at Wurzburg in Germany. This states that 'Mo-sinu maccu Min, scribe and Abbot of Bangor, was the first of the Irish who learned by rote the compactus from a certain learned Greek.' Compactus is a kind of ecclesiastical computation. The note adds that this ancient knowledge was written down by a pupil of Mo-sinu called Mo-Cuaroc maccu Neth Semon. Some experts suspect this makes Bangor the origin of the first Irish Chronicle, on which all the Annals of Ireland were later modelled.

The abbey's golden age ended abruptly in 824 AD when its vulnerability to sea-borne attack was ruthlessly exploited by Viking raiders. Some 900 monks were killed during looting and the shrine of St Comgall was stolen. From this date onwards Bangor never fully recovered and a succession of distinctly amateurish abbots – mostly laymen – presided over its decay. The building was briefly restored by St Malachy in the 12th century but when he was promoted to the See of Down it again fell into disrepair. Today nothing remains of this world-renowned centre for Christian scholarship apart from a stone structure known as Malachy's Wall.

Right: *Sunrise over Belfast Lough.*

'SOMEDAY YOU WILL BE OLD ENOUGH TO READ FAIRY STORIES AGAIN'

With mist-laden mountains, ice-cold lakes and crumbling castles, it's a landscape that inspires epic fantasies and extraordinary adventures. For author C. S. Lewis (1898–1963) the scenic high spots of Co. Down became the gateway to another world.

It was an entirely different dimension, where children talked to otters and fauns, where a goodly lion did battle with an evil queen, where it was always winter but never Christmas. It was, of course, Narnia, the enchanted land where the novel *The Lion, The Witch and the Wardrobe* is set.

The most familiar in a series of seven books, it parallels the Christian message and reflects the author's deeply-held faith. Yet put the religious imagery aside and it's still a remarkable yarn that has kept several generations of children in thrall.

When they were published in the Fifties the Narnia books attracted considerable literary criticism, not least by *Lord of the Rings* and *The Hobbit* author J. R. R. Tolkein. They have been attacked in the subsequent half-century for being racist, sexist, militant and more. Still, in excess of 100 million copies have been sold in 41 different languages to children who have all yearned to find a new crisp-air world lurking at the rear of their wardrobes.

He was born Clive Staples Lewis in industrial Belfast were his maternal grandfather was a Church rector. Nonetheless, as a boy and a young man he was a confirmed atheist – and was better known as Jack. He thrived on the freedom of the wild countryside outside Belfast and the numerous potent folk legends associated with Ulster.

Prodigiously talented, he abandoned an early scholarship to Oxford University to serve in the British Army in World War I. He was injured six months before the end of the conflict at the Battle of Arras and ultimately returned to Oxford where he stayed as student, tutor and professor until 1955 when he left for Cambridge.

Aged 31 he converted to Christianity and the topic became uppermost in his mind. But while the preface he wrote for a publication of Milton's classic 'Paradise Lost' is highly regarded, it is for the creation of Narnia that he is best remembered.

In all the years he spent in England he could never drum up enthusiasm for the English countryside, which he felt came a poor second to that of his native Northern Ireland. No surprise then when it came to drawing up a map to bring Narnia into sharp relief for readers that he fell back on what he loved best, the Mountains of Mourne. There were Neolithic burial mounds, mysterious standing stones, forgotten ruins and a sense that the magic riven through ancient sagas is about to bubble up through the lush grass. Its backdrop provided a lasting tribute to the place he always believed to be home.

Lewis and fellow writer Aldous Huxley died on 22 November 1963, the events entirely overshadowed by the assassination of American president John F. Kennedy.

Afterwards his brother Warren confirmed the author's commitment to the mountains of County Down: 'What he sighed for was the lost simplicity of country pleasures, the empty sky, the unspoilt hills, the white silent roads on which you could hear the rattle of a farm cart half a mile away.'

Left *Author C S Lewis incorporated the magical landscapes of Co. Down (**above**) into his children's tales.*

QUENCHING BELFAST'S THIRST

As business in Belfast boomed so the city's thirst for water multiplied. Anxious water company experts cast around for a ready supply – and found it in the Mountains of Mourne. An ambitious scheme that spanned sixty years was drawn up by Victorian engineers who could never hope to see it achieved.

Its first phase was a stone wall that stretched for 35 km (22 miles) enclosing 3,640 hectares (9,000 acres) bought by the Belfast Water Commissioners not so much for what the land could yield but for the rain that fell on it.

Work on the wall began in 1904 and lasted for 18 years, bringing much needed employment to the region. Following the contours of 15 mountains at an average of 2.2 m (8 ft) in height and 1 m (3 ft) in width, its completion was no mean feat and remains a magnet for visitors today.

Then came the prospect of building the reservoir earmarked for Happy Valley that would help provide 3,000 million gallons for Belfast. Although its first turf

was cut in 1923 problems with building the necessary retaining wall held up development for some time.

Even before the technological problems had been resolved a new town had been built in the mountains to house many of the 2,000 engineers, supervisors and workmen employed on the project. It provided 'home comforts' including a bar, cinema, café and even a policeman with the unlikely name of Lawless. A railway was laid to the site to carry in materials. With its own power station, Watertown had the first electric street lighting in Ireland.

It provided much needed employment in a now-flagging economy, which meant that some men still trekked in from their distant homes each day. The only alternatives for most were stone quarries or fishing.

However, the water project was completed at a cost of eight lives. One man, John Murphy, died shortly after accompanying the body of a friend back from Scotland where both worked in a colliery. His mother had begged him not to return to the mines, only for him to die in a tunnel collapse in 1929. Happy Valley became Silent Valley on the fairly spurious charge that wildlife had fled from the area.

The next phase in the water project involved tunnelling through Slieve Binnian, a process that meant the removal of 47,000 tons of granite. Two teams began work, heading from different sides of the mountain into the middle. Working conditions were atrocious with foul air and poor lighting. When they finally met in December 1950 there was barely a discernible difference in the tunnel bore that now stretched for 3 km (2.5 miles). It finally opened in 1952.

It wasn't the end of the project though, for a second reservoir was now needed at Ben Crom above the existing facility. This time pre-cast concrete was used rather than the hand-mixed variety that held the waters of Silent Valley. Work was completed by 1957.

In addition there were a series of conduits channelling water from rivers to quench the thirst of the city. Work on the project was not completed until the 21st century, a tribute to the foresight of the Victorian engineers behind its inception.

Opposite: *Atop Slieve Binnia, Co. Down.*
Below: *Water freely available in the Irish mountains is collected to satisfy the thirst of Belfast industry.*

HOMES AND CASTLES

Strangford Lough is a place of contrasts, nimble with wildlife and rigid with reach-for-the-sky castles. Some of the strongholds are luxurious while others amount to little more than rubble.

Perhaps the finest of the castles is Mount Stewart, bought by the first Marquess of Londonderry with rag-trade riches. It was the childhood home of Robert Stewart (1769–1822), who became one of Britain's most unpopular MPs.

Club-footed Stewart helped suppress the Irish rebellion of 1798 and did much to steer the 1801 Act of Union between England and Ireland through Parliament. Promises he made about Catholic emancipation came to nothing, however, with a regime change brought about by subterfuge on the part of King George III. Later, as Lord Castlereagh, he became closely associated with parliamentary repression, which culminated in the Peterloo Massacre of 1819 when peaceful protestors were charged by armed militiamen.

Booed in the street, Castlereagh became a target of abuse. After hearing about the Peterloo Massacre Percy Bysshe Shelley (1792–1822) wrote a protest verse which included the lines: 'I met Murder on the way – He had a face like Castlereagh.'

Public disdain seemed to affect the balance of his mind and in 1822 Castlereagh used a penknife to sever his carotid artery. At the time suicide meant burial at a crossroads with a stake through the heart. However, to enormous public outcry, Castlereagh was spared this ignominy when a jury decided he was insane.

Perceived as privilege once again playing its part in British politics, Castlereagh's coffin was jeered on its way to Westminster Abbey.

More rugged among the lough-side citadels is Kilclief Castle, built in the first half of the 15th century and the home of John Sely, Bishop of Down. He was ultimately evicted after it was discovered that he was living with a woman, Lettice Whailey Savage, whom he refused to give up.

Kilclief extends to four floors with a spiral staircase in one corner and a series of garderobes – or toilets – in another. A 13th century coffin lid was recycled to provide the lintel for a fireplace.

Still bearing splendid crenellations the castle has lost the thatch that apparently once topped it.

Audley's Castle, Sketrick Castle and Strangford Castle are among those that date from the 15th century too but haven't retained the fascias common to Kilclief. The sheer number of castles rubbing shoulders around the lough has much to do with John de Courcy (1177–1204) a knight made Earl of Ulster who had numerous skirmishes with Irish tribes before incurring the wrath of Prince John. A giant of a man with astonishing strength, it is said he was arrested on Good Friday, the only time of year when he divested himself of armour, while doing a penance at a church altar. Even then he killed 13 with a handy pole before being detained.

Given the era switch it's assumed that many of the fortresses were rebuilt, as Ringhaddy Castle was in 1602. Later still Castle Ward is a 17th century grand-scale family home, lavishly appointed inside and out with vistas enhanced by the loughs and its 120 small islands that are themselves attractive homes for birds and seals.

Homes and castles around Strangford Lough range from the bleak, such as Audley's Castle (above), to the stately, such as Mount Stewart House (opposite). It's likely the sites of most were established by an ambitious knight who subdued numerous local tribes at the dawn of the Middle Ages.

THE MOUNTAINS O'MOURNE

In some ways Percy French was a typical Irishman with a love of language, an ear for music and an easy sense of humour. Yet he was also at odds with the Irish stereotype, being from Protestant land-owning stock.

Even in his early life he composed music and amused himself by penning poetry that was irreverent and ironic although never rude. However, his father chose for him a career in civil engineering and it was to this end that he entered Trinity College, Dublin in 1872. It took him years to achieve the necessary qualifications because he devoted most of his time to writing verse, the most exceptional being *Abdullah Bulbul Ameer*, a satirical account of the Turko Russian war that became a music-hall hit. In his naivety, he failed to secure copyright for the song and so never received a penny for his effort or success.

Eventually, to his own amusement, he got a job as a 'drains inspector' in County Cavan. It was here that he began writing in earnest and also painting at which he was equally accomplished.

The dual distractions eventually meant he was 'let go' by his employers and he decided to try his luck as a comic magazine editor in Dublin. Alas, *The Jarvey* failed to prosper. Worse till, his wife Ettie died in childbirth and their daughter was dead a few days later.

French then turned to the theatre where his talents were ideally suited. He began a rootless life, marrying a second time and fathering two more daughters before moving to London. His lifestyle was glamorous, he even visited North America and the West Indies in 1910. Yet he was never entirely comfortable in high society, nostalgic for the simple ways of his native Ireland. He returned often to paint the inspiring scenery and enjoy the craic at local inns.

Despite a glowing reputation he was nonetheless taken to court for *Are Ye Right There Michael* by a vengeful West Clare railway company parodied in the song. French won the case after being late to court having taken the train.

The key to his success was his economy with words and an uncanny feel for the dilemmas facing working people. His song *The Mountains o'Mourne* forever links him with County Down where there's an exhibition devoted to him in Bangor. In its first verse the song is an affectionate prod at the artless Irish who went abroad in droves to find work while at the same time acknowledging their personal sacrifice.

Oh Mary this London's a wonderful sight
Wid the people here workin' by day and by night
They don't sow potatoes, nor barley, nor wheat
But there's gangs of them digging for gold in the street
At least when I asked them that's what I was told
So I just took a hand at this digging for gold
But for all that I found there I might as well be
Where the Mountains o'Mourne sweep down to the sea.

Opposite: *The breathtaking vista to the Mourne Mountains that so inspired Percy French.*

EDINBURGH

Presented by Rory Bremner

Rory Bremner provides expert comment on 'Auld Reeky' showing how its architecture, culture and long enlightened history rightly give it the sobriquet of 'The Athens of the North'.

MORNINGSIDE MADNESS

In Edinburgh's smart Morningside neighbourhood the peace is shattered after
a man finds his wife in a passionate embrace with his son from a previous
marriage. Her shrill screams echo as he stabs her in a jealous rage.

The killing of Elizabeth Pittendale years ago might have
been long forgotten if not for reports of her ghost,
known as the green lady, roaming in Balcarres Street –
the scene of the outrage. It's one of many spectre
sightings that have earned Edinburgh the title of Europe's
most haunted city.

Across town the blue lady – that is thought to be
accomplished actress Ellen Terry (1847–1928) – appears
sporadically at the Royal Lyceum Theatre while the
Edinburgh Festival Theatre is still apparently home to
illusionist Sigmund Neuberger, the Great Lafayette,
nearly a century after he died in a blaze on the site.
Neuberger was engulfed in flames when an oriental lamp

fell on his head in 1911 and perished alongside two
midgets from his theatre company. Although the
elaborate theatre was destroyed the audience escaped
without loss of life.

The castle, of course, has an array of ghosts including
a full complement of phantom pipers and drummers. But
perhaps the most haunting story involves a lone drummer
boy sent to investigate one of the tunnels leading from
the castle. He continually beat his drum so observers
could monitor his progress and he appeared to be
following the route of the Royal Mile, heading towards the
Palace of Holyroodhouse. Abruptly, the drum beats
ended and a search party that made tentative

investigations of the tunnel found no trace of him. However, even today the mournful sound can still be heard emanating from somewhere below ground.

Major Thomas Weir (1599–1670), a leading covenanter and captain of the guard in his native Edinburgh has also been heard but not seen. In old age he wore religious robes, leant on a blackthorn staff and preached across the city. Indeed, it was at a religious meeting that he began to confess extraordinary sins. He was guilty of incest with his sister Jean, he told astonished listeners, and also bestiality, having made a pact with Satan.

He was duly tried, found guilty of witchcraft and strangled before being burnt at the stake. Attempts to reduce the staff to ashes were almost thwarted when it allegedly assumed a life of its own and danced to evade the licking flames. It was the staff that was later seen at Weir's house, searching for its master. Meanwhile the sounds of revelry that came from the deserted house troubled neighbours. The house in the Bowhead area was finally pulled down in the 19th century yet partying can still be heard.

Meanwhile a doomed kitchen boy is walking Scotland's corridors of power. A mad aristocrat butchered the lad, roasted him on a spit and had begun to eat the body at Queensberry House in Canongate, now incorporated into the Scottish Parliament building. During celebrations of the 1707 Act of Union James Douglas, 3rd Earl of Queensberry (1697–1715) somehow escaped his locked room and committed the atrocity. The oven he used can still be seen in the Parliamentary Allowances Office.

Opposite: *Ghosts are thought to roam Edinburgh Castle.*
Below: *Holyroodhouse Palace was the apparent destination of an ill-fated drummer boy.*

ATHENS OF THE NORTH

Eighteenth-century Edinburgh was a smoky, vermin-ridden tenement city summed up in the title of a poem written by Robert Ferguson (1750–1774), *Auld Reekie*. Here, the rich rubbed shoulders with the poor – and the super-rich left for London.

To woo back moneyed Scots, who had found life south of the border more amenable, authorities displayed extraordinary vision in 1752 by orchestrating a city regeneration project. Breaking new ground to the north of the existing settlement, symmetrical streets, terraced town houses and spacious squares in discreet classical style were the order of the day.

The result was a delightful grid-iron neighbourhood rich with elegant circuses and crescents that duly lured back the émigrés. To satisfy their requirements, there also came a rash of libraries, publishing companies, legal firms, a university and medical school, changing the profile of the city entirely and bringing about Edinburgh's Enlightenment.

Initially this new town was separated from the old by Nor Loch, flooded marshland that was a favourite spot for witch dunking and suicides, murder victims and effluence. Its murky waters were finally drained by the 19th century and the site became the Princes Street gardens.

Despite its high winds, horizontal rain and shortage of sunshine, Edinburgh was dubbed the 'Athens of the North'. Nowhere was this aspiration more apparent that on Calton Hill, a tamed crag with the city rolling out

around it. On it there's a Grecian-style temple devoted to Scottish philosopher Dugald Stewart (1753–1828) and the Old Royal High School, built in 1829 to reflect the prevailing neo-classical culture. There's a tower in the shape of an upturned telescope marking Nelson's achievements in the Napoleonic era, along with two observatories, the most recent built in 1818.

Then there's the foundations of Edinburgh's own Parthenon. A stunning signature for a city skyline, there were ambitious plans to commemorate those Scots killed in the Napoleonic Wars by replicating the ancient Greek temple. Despite a respected architect, William Playfair, heading the project, money had run out by 1822 and the mighty platform bearing a dozen giant columns was abandoned. As memories of the Napoleonic Wars receded so did the desire to complete the costly landmark. Although it has charm, the half-finished folly for the war dead is known locally as 'Edinburgh's disgrace'.

Similar building projects were taking place at the same time in Munich which was also competing for the 'Athens of the North' sobriquet. Fortunately none of the buildings on Calton Hill, unfinished or otherwise, ruined the vista.

Robert Louis Stevenson believed Calton Hill was the best place to view Edinburgh 'since you can see the Castle, which you lose from the Castle, and Arthur's Seat, which you cannot see from Arthur's Seat.'

True, and it's also possible to see the Firth of Forth, renowned for its two bridges. The rail crossing came first, three distinctive sideways steel diamonds opened in 1890 at a cost of 57 lives and £3,200,000. With a surface area of 18 hectares (45 acres) it was being painted continuously for the first 100 years of its life until paint technology created an improved, more durable coating.

The road bridge, opened in 1964 at a cost of £19,500,000, was hailed as the largest suspension bridge in Europe.

The view from Calton Hill (opposite) *embraces the city in one direction and the Firth of Forth railway bridge* (above) *in the next.*

LITERARY EDINBURGH

Today Edinburgh's literary landscape is acclaimed as rich and varied. The man chiefly responsible for kick-starting it was Sir Walter Scott (1771–1832).

Born in Edinburgh's old town where insanitary conditions surely contributed to the death of five siblings, Scott himself contracted polio at an early age and left the city as a child for healthier climes.

But he returned to be educated at the High School of Edinburgh, then the university. Afterwards, for at least some of the year, he lived in Edinburgh in one of the newly built three-storey homes in North Castle Street.

As a writer he is best remembered for classics adventures such as *Rob Roy* and *Ivanhoe* and the 1810 Arthurian poem *The Lady of the Lake*. But his legacy goes broader and deeper.

In fact, Scott was instrumental in organising the 1822 visit to Edinburgh of King George IV, that helped reinvent the kilt, banned in polite society for its association with rebellion. Although Scott was an expert on the folk history of the Lowlands, he was liberal in his interpretation of Highland customs and tartan became an issue of fashion rather than clan. George himself donned a short kilt, despite his mighty girth, and a pair of tights.

Scott also popularised Celtic culture and his works were turned into operas, the influential entertainment of the day. In short, he turned the spotlight on Edinburgh in celebration of its renaissance.

Not everyone was enamoured with Scott, whose writing was branded ponderous and humourless. Mark Twain firmly believed that the romance he attached to battle beckoned the American South into Civil War.

But Scott will never be forgotten in Edinburgh where his monument – memorably described as a 'gothic sky rocket' – dominates East Princes Street Gardens, and the main railway station was named 'Waverley' for his popular historical novel.

Another towering literary figure Robert Burns (1759–1796) was a frequent visitor to Edinburgh. He clearly revelled in the liberal environment of the city, so much so that he fathered 13 children by five women before his death aged 37.

A generation later the literary scene was illuminated by Robert Louis Stevenson (1850–94), author of classic novels *Treasure Island* and *Kidnapped* and the famous short story *Dr Jekyll and Mr Hyde*. Although he left to escape its foul winters Scotland remained an inspiration in his writing and the Scottish-set novel *Catriona* was written from Samoa, where he died.

Sherlock Holmes' creator Sir Arthur Conan Doyle (1859–1930) and Muriel Spark (1918–2006) who wrote *The Prime of Miss Jean Brodie* were both born here.

Today the literary torch is being held by author J. K. Rowling, whose series featuring wizard Harry Potter has been a runaway success. She has lived in Edinburgh since returning from Portugal with daughter Jessica in 1994 and it's where she wrote much of the award-winning series. Other prominent authors linked with the city include Irvine Welsh, Ian Rankin and Alexander McCall Smith.

As a counterbalance, Edinburgh was also the birthplace of William McGonagall (1825–1902), recognised as the worst ever British poet. To show you why, here's the final verse of his ditty dedicated to the city.

Beautiful city of Edinburgh! the truth to express,
Your beauties are matchless I must confess,
And which no one dare gainsay,
But that you are the grandest city in Scotland at the present day.

Opposite: *A distinctive memorial to Sir Walter Scott in Edinburgh has been dubbed a 'gothic sky rocket'.*

FESTIVAL EDINBURGH

It started as a kind of cultural therapy to heal the scars left across Europe by World War II. Now the Edinburgh International Festival is vast and varied and swallows the city whole.

In 1947 an official summer programme of theatre and music was proposed and packed audiences were anticipated. At the outset some acts turned up uninvited, finding impromptu venues in which to stage performances. It was the birth of the Fringe, the *avant garde* face of the festival for which 1.53 million tickets were sold in 2006.

As the potential for the event was realised so there followed a book, film, television and jazz festival all running concurrently. At the same time the Edinburgh Tattoo takes place in the precincts of the castle, loud with cheers, pipes, drums, battle re-enactments and firecrackers. The Edinburgh Mela is staged for two days,

a spiritual and multi-cultural occasion to promote peace. All come under the umbrella of the Edinburgh International Festival.

The breadth and depth of the event – and the crowds – is breathtaking. The streets are hectic and accommodation is hard to come by. These days, most people come for the Edinburgh Festival Fringe.

For three weeks in August Edinburgh hosts the Fringe's 28,000 performances at 261 venues. In 2006 there were no fewer than 1,800 different shows to choose from, ranging from stand-up comedians through magicians and puppeteers to dance and drama. A goodly number of acts are performed free as

street theatre so there might be a juggler on one road junction, an acrobat on the next.

Of course, not all are brilliantly innovative. In fact, some are downright awful but there is no artistic vetting beforehand. Open access for all performers is one of the cornerstones on which the Fringe has been built.

It hasn't always been so. Until 1968 scripts had to be read and approved by the Lord Chamberlain's office. If rules curbing the artistic licence of particular productions were brought in, its performers typically went through hoops to sidestep them so the show could go on as intended.

Other criticisms have been levelled at the Fringe in recent years. It has been branded too professional, too unprofessional, too rude, too crude, too commercial, too big and too extreme. Still, record breaking audiences year after year tell a different story.

Despite its unwieldy size the Fringe is put into the shade in terms of audience numbers by the Military Tattoo. About 100 million television viewers share the experience every year. On display are the best of the Scottish regiments and every year they are joined by overseas guests thus far as diverse as a children's choir from Uganda, Cossack dancers from Russia, gymnasts from Estonia and a Kung Fu troupe from China.

Apart from the festival, visitors travel to Edinburgh in numbers to experience Hogmanay, Europe's biggest New Year celebrations. About 100,000 people crowd the streets, with entertainment provided on four open-air stages and by a mighty fireworks display at midnight. At the chimes, the song on everybody's lips is *Auld Lang Syne*, with lyrics by the great Scots poet, Robert Burns.

Opposite: *Edinburgh Castle's Military Tattoo is a grand ritual in the calendar.*
Above: *On street corners solo performers attract smaller crowds.*

ROYALS AND REBELS

Perched high on a rocky ledge, Edinburgh Castle is the lofty landmark that's an emblem to Scottish nationhood.

In one guise or another, it's been in existence since the Iron Age – possibly earlier. It was the home of the Scottish monarchs – except when it was in the hands of the English. Edward I – the hammer of the Scots – squatted there until his forces were overwhelmed by 30 supporters of Robert the Bruce who scaled the sheer sides of the castle's escarpment in an ambitious commando raid. Cromwell was the last unwelcome guest, poised to pounce on rebellious Royalists.

The oldest building on the site is a 12th century chapel dedicated to St Margaret, who died there in 1083, broken hearted after the death in battle of husband King Malcolm III. It underwent a series of improvements after winning royal favour, culminating with the great hall in 1511, built by James IV.

Had destiny been kinder to Mary, Queen of Scots, the castle may well have been the seat of even greater power. Aged 15 she married the heir to the French throne, uniting two longstanding enemies of England. But when her husband died the union ended and plans to squeeze England into submission and make Scotland the primary power were sidelined.

In 1566 she gave birth to son James within the walls of the castle, fearing for her safety having antagonized Protestants and Catholics. Misguidedly, she renounced the throne and fled to England where she was promptly imprisoned and ultimately executed. However, James grew up to be King of Scotland and England after Queen Elizabeth I died in 1603 with no other heir. The castle was at the centre of other skirmishes and its role inspired Robert Burns to lyrical rhyme.

There, watching high the least alarms,
Thy rough, rude fortress gleams afar;
Like some bold veteran, grey in arms,
And mark'd with many a seamy scar:

The pond'rous wall and massy bar,
Grim-rising o'er the rugged rock,
Have oft withstood assailing war,
And oft repell'd th' invader's shock.

Today it's a tourist trap although it still acts as an army headquarters. On show is Scotland's royal regalia, stowed away after the 1707 Act of Union and liberated more than a century later by patriot Sir Walter Scott. In quirky tradition, a single canon is fired daily at lunchtime.

As fortification intensified at the castle – and the amount of explosive stored within its walls increased – it became an altogether less desirable place to live. Consequently the royals moved down the road to Holyroodhouse Palace.

It began life as a monastery until the royals installed themselves. Afterwards its fortunes rose and fell, mirroring that of the monarchy. Holyroodhouse Palace was at its lowest ebb when Cromwell's troops were billeted there as it suffered extensive damage. During his visit, George IV called for improvements and Queen Victoria, enamoured of Scotland, carried out renovations. Today it is the home of the Queen when she is on official business, and is a busy working palace.

Opposite: *Today Edinburgh Castle is the destination of tourist battalions rather than ambitious invading armies.*

SLEEPING LION

Millions of years ago, as the earth was grinding out a landscape, the area around Edinburgh was blessed with high, wild vantage points.

Probably none is finer than Arthur's Seat, a long-extinct volcano that adopted the profile of a sleeping lion. It got its name in the 15th century, perhaps because King Arthur was said to have sat here to watch his army defeat the Picts. More likely it marks a different, more local hero who shares his name.

Lying about a mile to the east of Edinburgh Castle, Arthur's Seat rises to 251 m (823 ft) and offers a spectacular panoramic view of the region. The walk to it and the surrounding Salisbury Crags is relatively undemanding. Remarkable for being so close to the city and yet so uncultivated, it is like the Highlands in miniature.

Although its geology – basalt cliffs – and its age – 350 million years – are known, there's one mystery about Arthur's Seat that has yet to be resolved. In 1836 17 small wooden coffins each containing a carved figure were discovered there. There's no clue as to who was responsible or why. The only deduction observers have made is that the discovery mirrors the number of victims claimed by 'bodysnatchers' Burke and Hare.

Irish by birth, William Burke and William Hare met in Edinburgh when they shared lodgings. It was a time when the city's eminent medical schools were short of corpses, used by surgeons for teaching purposes in front of paying pupils. Outside the classroom human dissection was considered both shocking and degrading, therefore only the bodies of vile murderers were offered to the anatomists and there were too few of these to satisfy demand.

So a black market for bodies was created, with the night-time pursuit of graverobbing so prevalent in the city that bereaved relatives mounted round-the-clock guards on the recently buried dead.

Burke and Hare were not so much bodysnatchers, more cold-blooded murderers. They were drawn into the murky underworld in 1827 when they found a fellow tenant dead in bed. He owed money to Hare who decided the dead man could posthumously settle the debt in body parts. With help from Burke he transported the body to Edinburgh's Medical School.

Realising that this was a lucrative source of income and that grave-robbing was problematic and hard work, Burke and Hare began murdering suitable candidates for their cadavers. Victims were made senseless with whisky then suffocated so their bodies were unmarked.

Often the dead weren't even missed. But the suspicions of students were aroused when they recognised the body on the slab, on one occasion belonging to a prostitute whom they knew had been in rude health shortly before. The killing spree only ended when tenants found a body under the bed at Hare's house. By the time the police were called it had disappeared, only to turn up at the medical school.

Hare turned King's evidence and Burke was found guilty of murder. He was hanged in 1829 after explaining how the first body was found and admitting 16 subsequent murders. His body was duly dissected and the skeleton is still on display at the University Medical School. A pocket book was made of his skin, now on display at the Police Museum on the Royal Mile. Hare was released from custody and left Edinburgh for an uncertain future as pauper.

Opposite: *Arthur's Seat in the shape of a sleeping lion is often deemed to offer the best view of Edinburgh and its historic buildings.*
Right: *The Canongate Tollbooth, built in 1591.*

ISLE OF SKYE

Presented by Charles Kennedy

Charles Kennedy celebrates the land of his forebears, showing the raw, breathtaking beauty of this part of the British Isles, as well as the people who forge a living from it.

SKYE BRIDGE

Six thousand years ago Neolithic farmers were settled on the Isle of Skye, marking a presence there and on other Western Isles with stone circles and passage graves.

No one knows how they got to the island but it surely wasn't in the same grand style available today. Quite the best way to approach Skye these days is by steam train on the Jacobite line running between Fort William and Mallaig, one of the most picturesque rail journeys anywhere.

The line was built at the start of the 20th century and is distinguished by the Glenfinnan Viaduct, a fabulous feat of engineering with 21 arches at heights in excess of 33 m (100 ft) arrayed in a gentle curve. It's made of concrete, the choice of material causing some consternation at the time. The overriding fear was 'that it would prove a monstrosity, sufficient in ugliness to take away all the charm and beauty of the scene.' Fortunately, its graceful lines and stunning backdrop assured it of a warm reception although builder Robert McAlpine was thereafter known as 'Concrete Bob'.

Fans of Harry Potter will recognise it as the route taken by the red-liveried Hogwart's Express, in reality a 1937 locomotive, in four films.

Until recently the only way to access Skye was by boat, much as Norsemen had done for several hundred years after 700 AD. There were at most three ferries to choose from and all tended to be thick with traffic. It

was time to build a bridge to Skye, a plan that had been kicked around for a century by various governments but dismissed with the equation of high costs and low population.

Controversially the government of the day sought a private company to build and pay for the project, recouping the costs through tolls. When the bridge opened in 1995 islanders were horrified to discover the toll was almost as much as the ferry fare. Meanwhile one of the ferries had been withdrawn, so alternatives to the bridge were diminished.

Skye islanders began a unified campaign of civil disobedience by refusing to pay the levy on journeys to the mainland. Meanwhile toll collectors revealed they were subjected to torrents of abuse. There was a total of 500 arrests following non-payments and 130 convictions. One man even went to prison for a short spell.

By 2004 the toll was judged to be 14 times that of the Forth Road Bridge, for a fraction of the distance. Before the year had ended the Scottish Executive had purchased the bridge from its builder/operators and the reviled toll booths were instantly removed.

Islanders celebrated by beginning their Hogmanay celebrations on the bridge. Free to all comers, the bridge is now thought to greatly enhance the tourist trade upon which Skye now depends.

Boat travel remains vital, though, for it links Skye with near neighbours Rum, Eigg, Muck and Canna – that are together known as the Inner Hebrides – and more distant islands such as Lewis and Harris of the outlying Western Isles.

Above: *The bridge linking the Isle of Skye to mainland Scotland has had a short but chequered history.*

BONNIE PRINCE CHARLIE

Politics and religion are always a dangerous combination and for James II (1633–1701) the outcome was catastrophic.

After pushing a Catholic agenda in a largely Protestant country he was ousted by William and Mary of Orange, his son-in-law and daughter. Still, his descendants firmly believed they had a claim on the English throne and grandson Bonnie Prince Charlie acted on it, banking on allies known as Jacobites.

When he turned up at Eriksay in Scotland in 1745 the prince knew no Gaelic, limited English and was without armed forces. Promises of French support failed to materialise but undaunted he proceeded to raise an army to seize the throne, now in the hands of George II. To his supporters he was King Charles III, to his enemies 'The Young Pretender'.

After two surprise victories against Hanoverian forces he reached Derby in England where, despite his ascendancy, he misguidedly decided to retreat. He was defeated at the Battle of Culloden in 1746 and went on the run with a £30,000 bounty on his head.

As a fugitive being hunted by thousands of the king's men he returned to the Hebrides. He only evaded capture thanks to the ingenuity of Flora MacDonald, on Benbecula, who dressed him as an Irish servant, called him Betty Burke and rowed with him to Portree on Skye. There he stayed in a cave – for the ruling McLeods has sided with the British government – until his flight to the continent was arranged.

This adventure is captured in a song that links Bonnie Prince Charlie forever to Skye, even though his stay on the island amounted to just a few days. Although inspired by an old Gaelic number, the music and lyrics for *The Skye Boat Song* were in fact not written until 1884.

And Flora MacDonald was not so much a sympathiser but acted out of concern for fellow islanders who would have been in peril had the prince been found among them. For her troubles, she spent some time in the Tower of London before returning to Scotland. She married and

emigrated to North America where her husband was captured during the War of Independence. Later they both returned to Skye where she died in 1790 at the age of 68. She's buried near the ruins of Duntulm, allegedly in the prince's bedsheet.

Life dealt harshly with the prince who returned to Europe convinced he was the rightful king of England. In secret he visited England twice more but was unable to stir interest in his cause. He turned to drink and died in Rome in 1788 in a condition that was far from 'bonnie'.

Inevitably there were repercussions after his visit for the residents of Skye and the rest of the Highlands. The Jacobites, comprising both Catholics and Protestants, were now a spent force but the English authorities were nonetheless vengeful. Thousands were killed or taken prisoner. The Act of Proscription in 1746 forbade the wearing of tartan and prevented Highlanders from bearing arms, all but annihilating local identity. It was 40 years before the Act was repealed.

Opposite: *Monument to Flora Macdonald.*
Above: *Skye remains a picturesque haven, just as it was for Bonnie Prince Charlie.*
Right: *Duntulm Castle Isle. One time home of both the MacDonald and MacLeod clans.*

OF SHEEP AND MEN

At the time of the Jacobite rebellion the Highlands and islands of Scotland were peopled with busy farming folk living among kinsmen and labouring on the land.

Then came the Clearances, wholesale evictions that swept half a million people from their homes and livelihoods. Cultural terrorism that began with the Act of Proscription was finished by the Clearances and Scotland would never be the same again. Usually, landlord greed is given as the reason behind the Clearances, which occurred in waves between 1785 and 1886.

With changes in agriculture transforming farming, the owners of vast tracts of land saw more profit in sheep than in tenant farmers. One peak in clearance activity, 1792, was nicknamed 'The Year of the Sheep'.

Heavies using bayonets, coshes and arson forced residents of villages to take flight in undignified haste. The traditionally made homes walled with turfs or clay and thatched with heather, broom and bracken, quickly vanished into the landscape.

There's little doubt that the British hierarchy was seeking to dismantle the clan system that dominated Highland politics and had proved pivotal during Jacobite unrest. But what the Highlanders called Clearances the aristocracy – and sometimes clan chieftains – branded 'improvements'. Justifiably, they could claim they were keeping pace with the Agricultural Revolution, the effects of which could be felt across Europe.

Displaced people had stark choices. They could travel to the cities, join the British Army or emigrate to Canada or North America. Some landlords who were anxious about the plight of tenants even financed their emigration.

Indeed, the chance to make a new life overseas was popular among the poor, so much so that in 1803 legislation was brought in to control emigration on behalf of landlords fearful of being deserted entirely by workers.

Aside from the aggression of landlords, the residents of the quaint townships had good reason to leave. The Clearances coincided with a prolonged period of poor weather that decimated harvests. When the potato famine struck in the middle of the 19th century their problems became acute. The population of the Highlands was increasing while food became increasingly scarce and it was time to make tough choices. However, a new life in unknown territory wasn't the answer for everyone.

Those that remained were awarded different stretches of land, usually coastal, with few prospects for agricultural development. There were other opportunities to diversify, including fishing, kelping and weaving that all became associated with crofters' existence. Life was precarious and once again tenants found they had little protection from the ambitions of landowners.

On the Isle of Skye a long-running dispute about grazing rights escalated into rent strikes and finally, in 1882, the Battle of the Braes. The skirmish occurred when 50 Glasgow policemen sailed to the island to enforce the landlord's authority. About 100 men, women and children armed with sticks and stones took exception to the strong-arm tactics. The ensuing court case attracted plenty of publicity, which cast grasping landlords in a poor light. By 1886 the Crofter's Act was belatedly made law, offering protection rights to the smallholders who wanted to continue their way of life in the face of rampant profit drives.

Opposite and below: *Crofters and their cottages are still in evidence on Skye despite a troubled history.*

GAELIC CULTURE

As the Highlands and islands emptied following the Clearances a once-prevalent culture became marginalised. But reports of its demise proved premature as Skye became a bastion of Gaelic heritage.

The language is still spoken, its legends are oft repeated, and music that harks back to its Celtic beginnings is heard. Tradition is strong, typified perhaps by Dunvegan Castle which has been occupied by the same family since 1270.

Rearing up from sheer rock face, it's the seat of the MacCleod clan, boasting a 14th century keep, a 15th century tower and a 17th century hall. The crenellations that frill the outside walls today were a Victorian addition.

It hasn't always been plain sailing for the McLeods (motto: Hold Fast) who have been at war variously with the neighbouring McDonalds from nearby Duntulm Castle, with various Scottish kings, with the English and

among themselves. When the potato famine arrived the McLeods left for a spell as, like so many others, they were unable to feed themselves.

The fairy flag of Skye, on show at Dunvegen Castle, illustrates the potency of Gaelic legend. On first sight it falls way below expectations. It is a tatty cloth of indistinct colour that's ready to crumble to dust. But stories behind the swatch of material lend it magical significance. One insists it was taken from the fairy kingdom years ago, which is why the king of the fairies is an annual visitor to Dunvegen.

It's also said to be the war banner belonging to would-be Norse invader Harold Hardrada who was killed in

1066 by a victorious English army. (Alas, the Normans were amassing to the south and the sweet taste of triumph soon vanished.) Another version says it came back with knights from the Crusades.

We know for sure that it's silk, was once yellow, and came from the Middle East between the 4th and 7th centuries. However, it's impossible to tell whether, as per legend, it brought victory to the McLeods in battles in 1490 and 1580 after it was unfurled. The McLeods have just one more opportunity to use it before its enchantment quota is expended.

Homes such as Dunvegen need considerable upkeep and when the 29th Clan leader John McLeod (1935–2007) found that repairs to his leaking roof would cost in the region of £10 million he came up with an innovative idea: he was prepared to sell the Black Cuillin mountains, a striking and moody range that dominates Skye, to cover his renovation bill.

When it was announced in 2000 the suggestion caused outrage. Although McLeod insisted a 17th century charter gave him rights over the mountains, many questioned his ownership. Dubious behaviour by landlords was, after all, an unpopular feature of Skye history. Ultimately, no one came up with the cash for the mountains and the 22 km (14 miles) of coastline, two salmon rivers, campsite and sheep farm that were also part of the deal.

Three years later the mountains were gifted to a nation that still thought it already owned them, while complex arrangements were made to finance the house repairs that are still pending.

Above: *Eilean Donan Castle on the Kyle of Loch Alsh – once the home of the MacKenzies who feuded with the McLeods at Dunvegan Castle – is now a stopping point for tourists en route to Skye.*
Opposite: *Dunvegan Castle.*

SEA EAGLES OF SKYE

The swooping and softly shrieking white-tailed sea eagle – known in Gaelic as 'the eagle with the sunlit eye' – has become a regular sight on Skye.

It's a recent and welcome return for a species that was once doomed in Scotland. The sea eagle was persecuted to extinction during the 19th century and when a sole remaining albino female was shot in the Shetlands in 1918 it seemed that the shadow of its mighty 2.4 metre (8 ft) wing span would never fall on Scottish ground again.

However, a reintroduction programme begun in 1975 has brought the majestic raptors back to Scotland in general and Skye in particular. A quarter of the existing population lives on the island.

As its name implies, the bird is conspicuous for the white feathers in its wedge-shaped tail and its habitat of sheltered sea lochs and coastal forests.

Among early settlers the eagle was presumably revered as its bones were found in ancient graves in the Orkneys. Their population was once distributed over all of Britain and they reportedly picked clean the corpses left on battlefields.

Much later, though, superstition held that eagles inspired a lucky catch for fishermen and these took to using eagle fat as bait. Also, as shoots became big business in Scotland, so the predatory eagle was targeted for its habit of stealing game birds.

Young sea eagles from Norway were used to re-populate the Highlands, beginning on the Island of Rum. Slow to breed, it was 1985 before young were born and raised in Scotland. Skye led the celebrations in 2006 when the 200th bird born in Scotland took to the air in their skies.

Still the number of birds alive today falls short of 100. At the most, breeding pairs produced three eggs a year. The single biggest threat to their survival remains unscrupulous egg hunters who shin up to tree-held nests to enhance their glass case collections, despite prohibitive penalties.

If they survive the attentions of egg thieves there's a host of other dangers ready to ambush eaglets, so that up to 70 per cent do not survive the first year.

High winds make it difficult for birds to take flight. If they cannot fly, they do not eat. Young are vulnerable to attack by other birds of prey, to deliberately poisoned bait and diminished habitat.

They feed on fish, sea birds, ducks and small mammals but these are by nature lazy creatures, just as likely to perch by a shoreline watching for washed up carcasses, or to peck at roadside carrion or even steal fish caught by otters.

Skye visitors can take advantage of special hides on the island in which to observe these fascinating birds. Only the most fortunate will witness the stunning courtship of sea eagles, in which a pair cartwheels in the air with talons entwined.

A cousin of the American bald eagle, they are distinct from golden eagles for having stubbier tails. For identification each is tagged, a numbered red disc clearly noticeable on its wing. This is a big clue for amateur birdwatchers because the white tail feathers and pale head and neck that distinguish the white-tailed sea eagle from its golden brother are late in developing

Opposite: *Yellow-billed sea eagles soar and swoop on Skye where the landfall is ideal for breeding and hunting.*

IN THE SHADOW OF THE CUILLIN

When Skye lives up to its name of 'the Misty Isle' then its greatest assets are veiled in iron grey – and may be obscured for days at a time.

Erupting from the island is a breathtaking mountain range stained by gabbro and granite, earning it the name Black Cuillin. Fashioned by ancient glaciers, this is Britain's definitive alpine landscape that is solemn in hue and severe in gradient. One dizzy precipice gives way to the next in the twisting and continuous ridge that frames the southwest corner of Skye.

On a clear day, when clouds race behind their serrated peaks, it's impossible to miss these sleeping giants. If in doubt about the challenge that these formidable slopes present to climbers, consider for a moment some translations of their Gaelic names. There's *Am Bastier*, the executioner, *Sgurra Ghreadaich*, the peak of torment,

and *An Barbh-choire*, which means wild cauldron. Sir Walter Scott wrote of them:

A scene so rude, so wild as this
Yet so sublime in barreness.

Yet it is the lure of these hazardous mountains that entices numerous visitors to Skye's shores. The Black Cuillin possess 12 Munros, that is, peaks over 914 m (3,000 ft), the highest being Sgurr Alasdair at 992 m (3,235 ft). They derive the name from Sir Hugh Munro (1856–1919) who first catalogued Scotland's towering mountains and discovered there to be 284

of them. Munro-bagging has become one of the region's greatest attractions.

One of the Munros, Blaven, lies near a different range properly called the Red Hills but sometimes known as Red Cuillin. These have lighter undertones and, in shafts of sunlight, are even granite red. Among the Red Hills there are two Corbetts, the classification of mountain below Munro extending to peaks between 762 m and 914.4 m (2,500 ft and 3,000 ft).

Lying among the mountains are the fresh inky waters of Loch Coruisk, detached from the sea in the lee of the scree slopes. According to Sir Walter Scott the loch was 'exquisite as a savage scene'. Meanwhile in 1849 Rev Thomas Grierson described it as 'the most terrific scene I have ever witnessed... The rocks, which are completely naked, are very dark and metallic-looking, their surface being encrusted with crystals, which occasionally glance vividly in the rays of the sun; and there are huge blocks here and there, placed in the most singular positions.'

Of course, the high ridges can wreak havoc with the weather. Among the earliest tourists to Skye were Dr Samuel Johnson and companion James Boswell, both prolific writers, who visited in 1773. Despite the immensity of the Cuillin they summoned up little prose about the island although Johnson was moved to comment on the weather: 'It is not pleasing. Half the year is deluged with rain. From the autumnal to the vernal equinox a dry day is hardly known.'

It's tempting to believe that poor visibility induced by inclement weather left them without a clear view of the mountains for the duration of their stay, for usually the effect of the Black Cuillin on visitors is striking. Paul Theroux, the American travel writer, after visiting the Cuillin mountains, wrote in '*A Kingdom by the Sea*': 'I wanted to come here again with someone I loved and say, "Look."'

Below: *The Black Cuillin are the backbone of Skye, erupting from the island to form a striking peak silhouette.*

YORKSHIRE DALES

Presented by

Lesley Garrett

One of Britain's much loved and
celebrated areas of natural beauty,
as well as home to such natural
wonders as Malham Cove, Britain's
renowned opera singer showcases
its many attractions and views.

ORE-INSPIRING DALES

The Yorkshire Dales is a tilted plateau dotted with gritstone peaks and run through
by numerous waterways. Today everything that lies above ground is highly prized,
primarily soft-stone villages, bleak moorland, bubbling waterfalls and verdant hills
dotted with black-faced Swaledale sheep.

But it wasn't always so, because in their creation the
Dales were seared with lead, which brought about a
buoyant industry. Now, however, few remnants of it
remain, a crumbling chimney here, an overgrown shaft
entrance there. Only the most informed visitor is aware of
the subterranean toil that went on.

Romans were in the business of mining at Swaledale
although it is likely to have occurred previously, in the
Bronze Age. Money-conscious monasteries in the
vicinity held the mining rights so it certainly existed in
medieval times and Yorkshire lead roofed elaborate
French abbeys and the King's castle at Windsor.

Then mining flourished – and failed – during the
18th and 19th centuries, when miners sometimes found

evidence of a long-distant predecessor or 't'owd man' as
they would put it. When business was at its height
Swaledale and Arkengarthdale between them yielded as
much as 6,000 tons of lead a year.

For men, women and children it was a dismal life.
Although they were in effect self-employed after striking a
deal with landowners over mining rights, they were paid
for the amount of excavated material shipped back to the
surface, which was then sorted and ultimately smelted.
With a thin seam of lead ore – or galena – this could
amount to precious little.

After trekking miles they filed singly down narrow,
dark tunnels armed with picks, hammers and oak
wedges to crack through rock faces. With them they

also took candles and used clay to prop them up. Inevitably the air was foul and the conditions treacherous, particularly when underground rivers became swollen after heavy rain.

Miners, existing on a meagre diet of porridge and brown bread, were prone to lead poisoning, chest infections and rheumatism. One slip in the clogs they traditionally wore could mean death as they navigated the labyrinth of underground tunnels. Still, it's said the dales rang with the sound of their voices as they sang on the way to work. Curiously, they also knitted as they walked, as both men and women supplemented their incomes by producing woollen garments as part of an enduring cottage industry.

A dip in the price of lead in the 1830s led to a local crisis and, as small mines closed, the workers moved to Durham to work in the collieries, or even emigrated. As competition in the Mediterranean flourished so the Yorkshire lead mines faltered and the prospect of employment certainty lured many away to the cotton and woollen mills in subsequent decades. By the 1880s the Yorkshire lead-mining industry was finished. Since then nature has reclaimed much of its territory. But it's still possible to see bell pits, hand-dug holes which continued until a lead seam became evident. There are tunnel mouths, now perilous through lack of maintenance, and also hushes, or channels, scoring the countryside. These were left after miners dammed a spot and then broke the barrier, letting the accumulated water strip away the foliage and throw up evidence of lead.

Beneath Swaledale (**opposite**) *and Arkengarthdale* (**below**) *there once lay lead seams formed in the prehistoric era. Supplies were exhausted before the 20th century dawned.*

MALHAM COVE

One of Britain's greatest natural wonders, Malham Cove echoes with the resonance of a bygone age. An arc of craggy limestone cliff, it stands 80 m (260 ft) high and at first glance could be mistaken for an ancient quarry or amphitheatre. However, this magnificent edifice isn't man-made but is carved out by nature, specifically the glaciers that raked over the region during three ice ages.

Thousands of years ago Malham Cove probably looked something like Niagara Falls. Water tumbling over the top shaped its rim, with the heaviest force evident at its lip. A last gasp by the glaciers put paid to the waterfall although there were reports of cascading torrents there in the 19th century after bouts of heavy rain.

Below there's a fertile green plain cut with a shining path of river, once home to hippos, rhinos and hyenas who later gave way to reindeer and bison. Above the cove there's a remarkable cracked limestone pavement, each crevasse a micro-climate in which delicate and diminutive plants can thrive protected from marauding sheep by nature's cattle grid.

It's thanks to the ice age effect that this limestone pavement exists. When the ice finally withdrew it stripped the landscape back to limestone platforms but left deposits such as boulder clay that ultimately formed soil. Water erosion then sculpted distinctive blocks called clints and fissures, known as grykes, in which the soil settled.

As rock gardens gained favour in British gardens limestone outcrops were ruthlessly harvested and now serious effort is being made to preserve splendid specimens such as this.

Water sinks below limestone surfaces and consequently the area is awash with underground caves, many of which are submerged. Divers are making astonishing geological discoveries after venturing into this eerie and claustrophobic environment, including that of stalagtites and stalagmites whose existence has shuffled the date of Malham Cave's formation back by a few thousand years to a lowest order estimate of 26,000 years.

Its other worldly feel has made it an inspiration for writers and artists. Charles Kinglsey, who wrote *The Water Babies* when he lodged at nearby Malham Tarn House, suggested the dark lines on the limestone cliff face were left by chimneysweep Tom as he fell. The setting for the children's classic was in nearby Malham Tarn. Poet William Worsdworth was awe-struck by Malham Cove's immensity and pondered how it was made. 'Was the aim frustrated by force or guile, When giants scooped from out the rocky ground, Tier under tier, this semicirque profound?'

Poet and philosopher John Ruskin was entranced by it while his close friend, painter J. M. W. Turner (1775–1851), found it appealing. Nonetheless, his depiction of nearby Gordale Scar, bearing similar geological hallmarks, was outgunned by lesser known artist James Ward (1769–1859).

Modern writer Bill Bryson, who lived for a while in Malhamdale, said: 'I won't know for sure if Malhamdale is the finest place there is until I have died and seen heaven (assuming they let me at least have a glance), but until that day comes, it will certainly do.'

Opposite: *Malham Cove is an impressive work of art wrought by nature rather than by man, that has left writers and painters spellbound.*

GOING UNDERGROUND

With Yorkshire's potent combination of limestone and rain inevitably comes a honeycomb of caves, scores of them in underground systems that run for miles and are getting bigger by the day.

Caves are created by the mechanical action of water. Sometimes it is laden with stones that rattle through a watercourse, carving itself an ever-greater path. In Yorkshire the water becomes imbued with carbonic acid which eats away at the limestone once it lazily settles in the easiest route it can find heading south. With the end of every ice age the water table dropped and it was to this new low-lying level that rain quested to arrive.

A certain breed of visitor finds as much beauty below ground as there is above. Wound round with rope and bearing a head torch, small armies of pot-holers disappear beneath the earth in Yorkshire to follow the fall and rise of a stream.

When daylight is gone their ears are filled with the rumble of a distant running rivulet and close by the echoing drip of water at work, smoothing, scouring and shaping the rocks into slow-growing tunnels and caves.

There's the splendour of stalagtites and stalagmites emerging from constant sculpting of the shale layered in the ground. It was the Victorians who first stuck their heads below ground to find a fairyland of pillars that measured their age in millennia. And it was they who committed outrageous vandalism by chipping out rock formations to feature in the fashionable grottoes of London houses.

Alongside the caves there are pools, often an eerie blue because of the mineral content gathered over the ages. The rushing draught that fills the caves and corridors is not sufficient to ripple the eddyless water, although surface tension in this uncanny environment might still be shattered by drips.

With the cave systems at Long Churn there are names that chill the hearts of the wary, such as Cheese Press, Letter Box and Greasy Slab. Alum Pot is properly known as the Mouth of Hell. Despite protective gear and hard

hats, traversing the underground routes still involves some shin-scraping and elbow-banging antics.

Long Churn runs for 366 m (1,100 ft) at depths of 107 m (321 ft) and has caves suitable for both novices and seasoned pot-holers.

No one knows the extent of the caverns beneath the Yorkshire Dales and there's still a chance of stepping where no man has trodden before or finding a hitherto obscured cave, a prospect that warms the heart of the true adventurer.

Meanwhile, above ground the flora and fauna provide a different manner of natural beauty. Farmers have become alive to a stunning array of wild flowers that flourish under their custodianship. Now grazing patterns are beginning to change so that meadows are left alone until the summer months when the flower heads have dropped, while animals return to different pastures prior to the plants' emergence. Native cattle rather than sheep are unleashed on these areas as they tend to be less brutal with plants. Further, they tread seeds into the ground, ensuring another fine display the following season.

Over centuries wild watercourses have bored into fragile limestone to create underground caves and tunnels, such as Gaping Gill (opposite) and Alum Pot (above), and remarkable stalactites, such as those in this Ingleborough cave (right).

SETTLE TO CARLISLE RAILWAY

Perhaps the most scenic train journey in Britain, the line scythes through moorland and peaks to provide an inspirational vista for travellers. Not everyone looked on the views with affection, though. For the navvies who built the line by hand for six years starting in 1869 the views were little consolation as they died in droves.

Frequently drenched in rain, many of the 6,000 workers perished in numerous accidents, particularly during the construction of more than 20 viaducts and 14 tunnels. There was one death a week at Ribblehead alone where the 24-arch viaduct stands 31.5 m (104 ft) high, every sixth arch being specially strengthened.

And they lived in hastily built shanty towns named for Crimean battles, such as Inkerman and Sebastopol, or for biblical locations including Jericho. Accommodated at close quarters the men were felled by an epidemic of smallpox as it ripped through the camps. The casualty rate was so great that the Midland company building the railway paid for an extension to the graveyard of a church en route.

In addition to the cost in human lives the bill for the project when it opened in 1876 was a mighty £3.6 million. Local people wondered if it was worth the expense, the stations often miles from their homes.

But this was a line built for speed so trains could compete with those on the existing West Coast line, at the time run by a competitor company. Engineers were briefed not to exceed a gradient of 1:100 so the line clung

to the landscape for its 116 km (72 mile) duration that includes the highest mainline station in England at Dent.

This was the last major line built in Britain and when buses and then cars became popular, passenger numbers dropped. Freight transport tonnage also plummeted and when the West Coast line was electrified in 1975 the route seemed doomed.

But its supporters rallied and saved the line not once but twice from closure. Why does a railway line have devoted fans? Well, this route goes among the famous Three Peaks – Whernside, Ingleborough and Penyghent, defining the essence of the Dales. Ribbledale viaduct, once known as Batty Moss, is curved so passengers can see the engine – usually diesel but sometimes steam – coming into view as they proceed. And at Ais Gill the line reaches its full height of 356 m (1,169 ft).

Train passengers understand why Yorkshire has become a sought-after film location for movies such as *Calendar Girls*, the 2003 film following the exploits of those in Rylstone Women's Institute who posed nude to raise cash for charity.

The calendar plan was hatched when the husband of one woman was dying from leukaemia. In a riotous send-up of themselves women of all ages and sizes agreed to pose without clothes, their privacy protected by props from a typically WI pastime, for example, cooking and gardening.

In short, the calendar got a rousing reception and raised £600,000. Disney wanted to film the incredible story. Although not all the women involved were convinced, the movie was duly made with Helen Mirren and Julie Walters. It was a warm-hearted, fictionalised account of what went on but for many the country towns and rolling countryside were key to their enjoyment. It was filmed in Kettlewell, Buckden, Burnsall, Ilkley and Malham.

Opposite and above: *The picturesque rail route that connects Settle to Carlisle. Although the exact death toll isn't known scores of men died as they hand-built the railway.*

COTTAGE INDUSTRY

Fashions come and go – and for that fact the people of Muker are grateful. Without the changing face of fashion a cottage industry that prospered hundreds of years ago might never have been revived.

The vogue for knitted stockings came in the wake of Queen Elizabeth I, who sensibly wrapped her royal legs in a pair when she was subject to fierce castle draughts. In the Yorkshire Dales, where there was wool in abundance, men, women and children began knitting stockings to generate some extra cash.

Afterwards there were fads for knitted garments, then there was the necessity for warm gear among people whose homes were rarely cosy. The people of the Dales knitted, some times more frantically than at others, to fulfil the demand. By the 18th century an estimated 18,000 pairs of stockings were produced each year in Swaledale. Yet it was only ever a profitable side line. The knitters had other jobs too, including farming and mining. Still, boys learnt it at their mother's knee and women could complete a sock en route to market.

But with the advent of the 20th century came the end of lead mining and knitting machines were killing off the demand for hand-knits everywhere. Dales folk put away their knitting needles convinced the era was at an end.

However, in the 1970s when economic depression brought villages such as Muker to the brink of extinction,

someone had the bright idea of reviving the hand-knitting industry. Villagers – many of them descendants of the knitters of yesteryear – would knit as they had been taught in childhood and their produce would be sold through a single outlet, Swaledale Woollens.

It was sound sense in an area where a sheep can be sheared in as little as 40 seconds. A single shearer can trim fleeces from at least 150 animals in a day, sometimes even double that number.

The Dales were receiving some helpful publicity thanks to *All Creatures Great and Small*, the book by James Herriot which was filmed and made into a television series. Having a woolly jumper from the region was considered high style.

Furthermore, the knitters used the highly insulating off-white wool from Swaledale sheep so naturally it was here that Sir Ranulph Fiennes turned when he needed 125 pairs of gloves for a polar expedition.

So the cycle of fashion paid dividends for Muker which has just 80 houses. Given its size it is surprising to learn the village has a silver band that plays across the country. In 1897 it was formed to mark Queen Victoria's Diamond Jubilee. Instruments were purchased with £52 raised by public subscription and Rev. James Cooke, the man behind the band, invited the leader from neighbouring Gunnerside band across to tutor musicians.

Today Gunnerside band is no more, although there is a brass band in nearby Reeth. There's little doubt that Muker Silver Band's stirring sounds, even in infancy, did much to support a society devastated by the loss of lead mining.

Opposite and above: *Making the most of its natural assets, Muker has maintained its picturesque beauty and dusted down its almost-forgotten hand-knitting industry to avert the economic disasters often associated with remote rural outposts.*

'AMBIENCE OF PEACE'

Vikings came to Yorkshire for raiding and trading purposes. In our mind's eye these were horn-helmeted warriors who rampaged across parts of England and France in terrifying style. But that's not entirely true as invading was only a part-time occupation. Their day job was farming – and they were good at it.

No one knows just why Vikings deserted their Scandinavian homes at the clarion call of a local leader. Certainly they possessed a hero ethic that inspired them to great adventure, and the prospect of plunder was, of course, enticing; also the ships they used were technologically brilliant so the journey was safe enough.

By 866 AD they were in control of York, previously the domain of Romans and then Saxons. Ivar the Boneless was leading the marauders having already killed King Edmund the Martyr in eastern England. Edmund it was who contrived Ivar's father Ragnar Lodbrok's death in a snake pit. So the Saxon Eoforwic gave way to the Nordic Jorvik and they peppered the place with Viking artefacts that have been uncovered in later years.

Still, we don't know what occurred outside the wealthy city. More than 500 fragments of Anglo-Scandinavian carving have been found around Yorkshire, mostly cross shafts and grave covers. However, whether the visitors colluded with Christianity or subverted it with pagan imagery isn't known for certain.

However, linguistics lead us to believe they made a home in Swaledale and were the forefathers of the region's farmers.

Gunnerside is derived from the Viking language and means slope or pasture that belonged to a Norseman called Gunnar. Keld is another Viking word, translating to spring, while Muker is yet another, meaning acre or small plot of land.

At the time of the Vikings there were no ropes of drystone walling around Swaledale. That came much later in medieval times at the instigation of monks from Fountain Abbey, who raised money from most of the land in these parts, and again in the 16th and 17th centuries, following enclosures. This was when landlords staked their claims to common land in a nationwide land grab, squeezing the smallholder.

The ruins known today as Crackpot Hall were unknown in Viking times. But perhaps the stone building replaced a Viking one. In 1298 the place was called Crakepot and its name derives from the Old English 'Kraka', a crow, and the Viking word 'Pot'. A 'pot' was usually a cavity or deep hole often in the bed of a river, but in Crackpot's case, refers to a rift in the limestone.

Once it was a grand and romantic shooting lodge from which the aristocracy would emerge to loose off some shots at the deer that once roamed here. Later it was a farm but now it amounts to little more than a pile of stones.

But for author James Herriot – also known as Alf Wight (1916–1995) – it was one of the highlights of Swaledale. Wight was brought up in Scotland and moved to Yorkshire in 1940 to begin a lifelong love affair with the place and the people, of whom he draws affectionate pen portraits in his best-selling books. In a book he wrote about Yorkshire he had nothing but superlatives about the Dales. Yet Crackpot comes in for special mention as '...nowhere is the Dales ambience of peace and mountain air so strong as in that country above Crackpot Hall'.

Opposite: *Once a luxurious shooting lodge, Crackpot Hall has become a ruin that serves as a landmark for hikers and a reminder of Viking heritage in Swaledale.*

THE GOWER

Presented by
Katherine Jenkins

This ancient land of Celts can rightly
be showcased as an area of not
only outstanding beauty, but one
of poetry, song and traditional Welsh
culture as shown by new singing
sensation Katherine Jenkins.

LA DIVA ADELINA

She was, quite simply, the greatest singer the world had ever known. Prima donna Adelina Patti had the world at her feet – yet she chose to live in a corner of Wales little known to anyone beyond Swansea.

La Diva Adelina performed in front of all the world's pre-eminent leaders including Queen Victoria, King Edward VII, Alexander II of Russia, Napoleon III of France and President Abraham Lincoln.

She was adored by the famous composers of the day. Guiseppe Verdi (1813–1901) believed her the greatest singer ever heard, and she sang at the funeral of Gioachino Rossini (1792–1868) as a mark of the bond that existed between them.

Unlike other singers of her generation, she was captured in song on Edison's phonograph. By 1905 when the recording was made the finer qualities of her vocal range had deteriorated somewhat. Nor does the primitive machinery do justice to her sounds. Yet through the historic recording it is still possible to discern the indisputable talent that gave her highly elevated status.

Born Adela Juana Maria Patti in 1843 to Italian parents in Spain she was the fourth of six children. It was a musical family with both parents and two sisters working as professional singers. Brother Carlo went on to become a conductor but they were by no means rich.

She spent her childhood in The Bronx where, it seems, she honed the range and quality of her coloratura soprano voice. Upon her New York debut in 1859 at the age of 16 there was a glimpse of the acclaim to come. Two years later she performed in Covent Garden, London, and made the city her base during a globe-trotting career. Among the highlights was a rendition of *Home Sweet Home* for Abraham and Mary Lincoln shortly after the death of their son Willie, which afterwards became something of a signature tune.

Known for her sharp business sense she commanded immense appearance fees and could have lived anywhere in the world she chose. However, in 1878 she purchased Craig-y-Nos in Abercrave (Abercraf) outside Swansea for a princely sum of £3,500. And she proceeded to spend a staggering £100,000 on improvements, including a clock tower, north and south wings, a glazed winter garden with tropical plants and birds and a theatre frequently used for private performances. Inside there was electricity – barely used in British homes at the time – and grand pianos in every room.

There was a private road to the local station at Penwyllt where a specially designated, luxuriously appointed waiting room was built. She even had her own train carriage for journeys.

She clearly loved the gentle beauty of Craig-y-Nos. It was here that she spent apparently happy years with second husband Ernesto Nicolini although her third husband, Baron Rolf Cederstrom, a Scandinavian 26 years her junior, clipped her wings.

In 1914 she gave her final performance to aid the war effort. Four years later she presented the fabulous winter garden to the people of Swansea. When she died a year later her body was soon transported to Paris for burial and her beloved house was sold.

Opposite: *Adelina Patti, who kept audiences agog with her astonishing vocal dexterity, loved the harmonious peace surrounding Swansea.*

CELTS AND CHRISTIANITY

In pre-Roman times southern Wales was colonised by the Celts, a legendary and fearsome crew who possibly bequeathed their best points to today's Welsh.

They may have been blue with woad and burdened with the heads of enemies severed in battles but the Celts also enjoyed words and song.

According to one 1st century Roman commentator: 'They have also lyrical poets whom they call Bards. They sing to the accompaniment of instruments resembling lyres, sometimes a eulogy and sometimes a satire.'

Let's put other descriptions he used – such as 'terrifying in appearance' and 'boasters and threateners' – to one side for now and be content in the likelihood that the Celts gave the Welsh a taste for colourful legends and a talent for singing, as testified by numerous all-male voice choirs.

Yet some of the pre-Christian monuments that pock the Gower were already in place on their arrival. Arthur's Stone, a massive boulder measuring 4 m by 2 m by 2 m (12 ft x 6 ft x 6 ft) on an 8 km (5 mile) sandstone ridge is dated 2,500 BC. It seems certain to have been a burial chamber, with the locals – whoever they were – excavating beneath it and inserting uprights.

It is said to be haunted by the ghostly apparition of King Arthur on a white steed. The roots of its association with Arthur may be in a poem by the Welsh bard Aneinin that told the story of a great hero written in 594. Perhaps significantly Art was the Celtic word for bear and the bear was a Celtic god.

Another ancient burial site is Giant's Grave, a long chamber and cairn, which once held 40 people entombed over several generations as well as Neolithic pottery. Forty bodies were already in Culver Hole, a landmark cave used in the Middle Bronze Age. Much later, it was a bolt hole for smugglers who were active on the Gower peninsula at the turn of the 19th century.

Of iron age forts, coinage, Druids and battlegrounds there is little evidence in the Gower. But the Celtic influence on early Christians is plain to see. Many early saints visited, lending their names to local churches established as early as the 6th century. This influx of Christian travellers overwhelmed the Celts and the traditions merged. St Cenydd, for example, was a local boy, born in the 6th century with a withered leg, cast adrift in a basket, rescued by gulls and reared by angels. He grew up to found St. Cenydd's Priory at Llangennith which later became a church and now has possession of a 9th-century Celtic wheel cross.

At St George's Church in Reynoldstone there's a pillar cross from 900 AD, rich with Celtic art. It was discovered in a field in 1800 and stood outdoors before being taken into the shelter of the church. St Illtyd is remembered in two Gower churches. The one in Oxwich Bay might even be based on a 6th-century Celtic cell.

What is certain is that the Celts gave the Welsh their lyrical language, more widely spoken now than for many years. Linked by its Celtic roots to Cornish and Breton rather than to Irish or Scottish, it evolved into the Welsh tongue between 400 and 700 AD.

Opposite: *Arthur's Seat.*
Above left: *Culver Hole, a former smuggler's hideout built into the cliffs.*
Above right: *St Mary the Virgin Church.*

SHIPWRECKS

Every coast has a history of shipwrecks, the evidence of which is swiftly lost to turbulent tides. However, reminders are dramatically marked out in the sand on the Gower peninsula where skeletons of lost ships pierce the beaches.

The most prominent of these carcass memorials lies in Rhossili Bay and belongs to the *Helvetia*, a Norwegian barque laden with a cargo of wood.

On Hallowe'en night in 1887 the ship was nearing the end of its voyage from Canada to Swansea when a calm autumn evening was shattered by the sudden descent of a roaring storm.

Although a companion ship reached safety in the lee of Lundy Island, the *Helvetia* was first stranded on a sandbank and then swept helplessly around Worm's Head on to the sands of Rhossili Bay. Fortunately no lives were lost despite the fierce gale. However, it proved impossible to free the ship from the grasping sands and there it remained. The wood she carried was unloaded, again in treacherous conditions. A boat that

returned later to collect an anchor lost during the operation was tipped over, killing seven aboard.

Helvetia's cargo was auctioned at rock bottom prices and rumours that Rhossili people had clad the insides of their homes with the timber abounded. Its framework now stands as a stark reminder, even on calm and sunny days, of the potential for treacherous winds and merciless seas here.

In different weather conditions the crew might have spotted the remains of *The City of Bristol*, a 210 ton paddle steamer that went aground close by in 1840. Seventeen crew members, seven passengers, 100 pigs and 18 cattle spilled into the swirling seas. Only two people were saved, one of whom was towed to shore on the tail of a surviving cow.

These are just two visible reminders of many dramatic events that have occurred off the coast. Of course, efforts have been made to prevent accidents. In 1794 the coal-fire beacon of Mumbles lighthouse was lit for the first time. Five years later beams from a single oil lamp were reflected across the environs. Manned until 1934 the lighthouse and its changing technology undoubtedly averted numerous tragedies.

And after 1835 the Mumbles possessed a lifeboat housed at various locations. Although initially its success was uncertain it notched up some sea-faring triumphs punctuated by several notable tragedies. In 1883 four crew members were lost when the lifeboat *Wolverhampton* was tossed against the side of the German barque *Admiral Prinz Adalbert*. Two of the dead were sons of coxswain Jenkin Jenkins. In 1903 six men were lost near Port Talbot, while in 1947 eight crew from the *Edward, Prince of Wales* lifeboat died alongside 31 crew of the *Santampa*, the ship in distress they were trying to assist.

The flip side to this courage comes in the form of the wreckers of Rhossili, supposedly at work during the early 18th century and compelled to kill shipwreck survivors so they could claim the salvage. Perhaps wreckers lured an unknown treasure ship to its doom during the 18th century, the cargo of which famously turned up during a low tide during 1807 and again in 1833. Local people still peruse the exceptional tidelines in the hope of recovering gold and silver coins.

Opposite: *Wreckage embedded in the sands of Rhossili Bay is evidence of the treacherous potential of the coast.*
Below: *Look-out stations and life-saving equipment posted around the coastline, including the Mumbles lighthouse, have saved many seafarers from the perils of treacherous currents and hidden sandbanks.*

GOWER NIGHTINGALE

Remote it might be but the Gower has an array of cultural quirks to call its own. Now a rearguard action is being fought so this heritage doesn't sink without trace into the peninsula sands.

Like most parts of the British Isles the Gower attracted the interest of Norman conquerors after 1066. Ultimately the new overlords transported people from Somerset to live on one coast and the area split into English Gower and Welsh Gower. The curious division of a rural outpost meant local customs were maintained on a parochial basis.

Traditions were handed down at the fireside by word of mouth. Little or nothing was written down and there's no source book available to illuminate their history or application.

One that occurs in several localities is the decorated horsehead borne at Christmas to households by crowds of revellers in search of food and drink.

It is known that the Mumbles horse head belonged to Sharper, a carthorse that once delivered fruit and vegetables around the area. Like other horses' heads – and one ram's head – used in the doorstep festivities, it was stripped of flesh and wired so that its mouth moved. Rather like today's 'trick or treat' visitors, the bearers of the horsehead stayed put until they were rewarded. Those householders who were slow to hand out goodies were chased around their kitchens by the skull's snapping jaws, the stuff of nightmares for the under fives.

Another Christmas tradition took the form of a Mummers play with characters including a Turkish Knight, a doctor, St George and Father Christmas. The performers wore white trousers and were bedecked with spotted ribbons. At New Year in Gower children put oranges on sticks and decorated them with holly, cloves and ribbon. If oranges were unavailable then a potato would do.

In November some Gower residents celebrated All Souls Day by trekking around households to sing a *Souling* song. Women made souly cakes for their visitors while men gave out small bags of wheat. Eventually donations of cash became more prevalent.

Most occasions like this were marked with a song and just about all have been sung by Phil Tanner (1862–1950), known as the Gower Nightingale. He was a folksinger of extraordinary quality who helped prolong the life of ballads that were fading into obscurity even in his lifetime.

The youngest of seven children, his father was a weaver and both parents along with other siblings had a talent for singing. Although he also worked as a weaver in his youth he eventually became a farm labourer. Aged 24 he married a 50-year-old widow in Whitemoor, the landlady of the Welcome to Town Inn. Presumably it was here that his public performances began, not just with song but also story-telling and mimicry.

Two recordings of Phil Tanner were made before his death and cultural historians have pored over the words and phrases of his songs for clues as to their origin.

Alas there's no footage of him as a wedding bidder, the Gower equivalent of an invitation. He went from house to house, usually mounted on a white horse with a staff festooned in white ribbons, repeating the bidding rhyme to each resident. The rhyme was not only a wedding invitation but also described the fare and entertainment that would be on hand for guests.

Opposite: *The Gower is rich in tradition and Phil Tanner, the Gower nightingale, ensured that old rituals and rhymes survived the test of time.*

DYLAN THOMAS

Born and brought up in urban Swansea, poet Dylan Thomas (1914–1953) looked to the sands of the Gower peninsula for inspiration from nature. It was, he said, 'one of the loveliest sea-coast stretches in the whole of Britain.'

He went from the Welsh back streets to international stardom, fêted as a celebrity wherever he went. Yet the influences of Swansea, the Gower and its environs remained evident in his words.

Before international travel beckoned he often spent whole days 'walking alone over the very desolate Gower cliffs, communing with the cold and the quietness'.

As a young man he went to Swansea Grammar School, where his father DJ was a literature teacher. After leaving he joined the local newspaper but it was friendships made at the Kardomah Coffee House and an association with the Swansea Little Theatre Company that resonated.

He left a short-lived career at the newspaper to concentrate on writing poetry. Busily he filled his 'Notebooks' with thoughts, phrases and ideas. It's thought as much as two-thirds of his entire poetic output occurred in his late teens.

In 1933 he saw his work published for the first time outside Wales, in the *New English Weekly*. A year later he moved to London to further establish his career. By now he was disenchanted with the ties that bound

him. 'Wales is the land of my fathers,' he said. 'And my fathers can have it'.

Still, perhaps the work that best defines Dylan was yet to be written, and it was penned in Laugharne, Camarthenshire, around the corner from his beloved Gower. He lived there off and on after 1934 when he became beguiled with the place, typified by the idiosyncrasies such as a converted Rolls Royce car which sold fish and chips.

After 1949 Dylan lived in the Boathouse in Laugharne 'sea shaken on a breakneck of rocks' with wife Caitlin and their three children. He could do so thanks to patronage from Margaret Taylor, wife of eminent historian A. J. P. Taylor, who picked up the bills. Largely a happy time – he wrote in glowing terms about the charm of Laugharne and its 'sane disregard for haste' – it was nonetheless the scene of alcohol-fuelled rows between Dylan and Caitlin. His plan was for 'a piece, a play, an impression for voices, an entertainment out of the darkness, of the town I live in, and to write it simply and warmly and comically with lots of movement and varieties of moods, so that, at many levels, you come to know the town as an inhabitant of it.'

The result was *Under Milk Wood*, the tale of townsfolk in their daily activities as well as their subconscious desires. Set in the fictional Llareggub (read it backwards) it became a sensuous story executed with skill, compassion and empathy.

Actor Richard Burton, fellow Welshman and the most famous narrator of the play, insisted 'the entire thing is about religion, the idea of death and sex'. Part of the skill was in writing so adeptly for the new medium, radio, with which he worked during World War II.

He delivered the script to the BBC before leaving for America. Although he died in New York his body was brought back to Laugharne for burial. If he wrote an epitaph for himself it was 'One: I am a Welshman; two: I am a drunkard; three: I am a lover of the human race, especially women.'

Opposite: *Natural splendours of the Gower fed Dylan Thomas sublime inspiration.*
Above: *Laugharne Castle, where Dylan Thomas wrote many of his works.*

FIRST VISITORS

Given its gorgeous views it comes as no surprise to learn that people have been visiting the Gower or Gwyr for centuries. In fact, the earliest tourists were there 28,000 years ago when early modern man roamed in the rolling hills.

He came to the Gower at a time when it was still attached to Europe by a land bridge where he lived – and died – among wild animals including hyenas, mammoths and bears. How can we be sure? Well, thanks to an extraordinary archeological find made in 1823, coupled with modern carbon-dating technology, we can draw an outline picture of Stone Age Wales.

The discovery was in Paviland Cave, a pear-shaped cavern lying in a Gower cliff face, by Reverend William Buckley, Professor of Geology at Oxford University and later Dean of Westminster. He discovered human bones coloured red with ochre tucked beside the cave wall. Other items nearby included jewellery and a mammoth skull. In fact by the time the excavation was complete 5,000 artefacts had been sifted from the shingle. A devout Christian, Buckley knew with certainty that no humans survived the Great Flood and concluded that this was the body of a prostitute from Roman times. She was called the Red Lady of Paviland and as such her fame spread across the world.

Only later did the truth emerge, that the she was a he who pre-dated classical times by quite a margin. He was about 175 m (5 ft 10 ins) tall, aged at least 21 and a hunter whose diet included fish. For unknown reasons he was buried with dignity and ceremony. The mammoth skull was emblematic while articles such as pierced shells and fox canines, polished sections of mammoth tusk and numerous flints were placed on the body by way of tribute. But if he had been a man of consequence while he lived, this was nothing to the significance he assumed following death. For even today he remains an outstanding scientific resource for an era about which little is known.

He had been in Wales during a window in the Ice Age when warmth made the valleys habitable. The cave in which the body was found was not next to the sea but above a fertile plain at a time when the River Severn ran at little more than a trickle. However, as the glacial climate crept closer, once more the plain turned into a polar desert and mankind's occupation of the landscape came to an end for perhaps 10,000 years. He has retained the name of the Red Lady of Paviland despite its obvious inaccuracy.

The cave is now cut off by a high-swelling tide that has scythed a path through the limestone cliffs and ribs beneath. The relentless grinding sea has produced another geographical feature for which the Gower is famous and that is sand, so abundant that it swamped a 6th century monastery in Rhossili Bay. The remains of the building, finally evacuated in the Middle Ages, can still be seen today. St Mary's Church was subsequently built on higher ground.

Opposite: *Carboniferous limestone cliffs line the glorious Gower coastline.*

ST IVES

Presented by Rolf Harris

Rolf Harris studies the impact of mining on the Cornish landscape; and the influence, in history, culture and economics, this remote area of Britain has had on our society.

AGE OF THE TINNERS

Look down any hole, anywhere in the world, and you'll find a Cornishman digging metal. At least that's what they'll tell you in West Cornwall and given the area's 4,000-year-old love affair with tin it's easy to see why this outpost of the Industrial Revolution has won global recognition for mining know-how.

The huge influence of tin mining on the Cornish landscape is impossible to miss. From winding houses on exposed cliffs to long-overgrown tramways and chimney stacks rising incongruously above the A30, there's barely a corner of the county that hasn't at some point been trialled for ore. The legacy of this remains a major headache for house-buyers because thousands of shafts and tunnels were never properly mapped or, if they were, those maps are long lost. If the words 'risk of subsidence' unnerve you, don't buy a property in Cornwall.

The Ancient Britons and Romans were the first to dig for copper and lead in these parts but it wasn't until the mid-19th century and the invention of the high-pressure steam engine by local engineer Richard Trevithick that the industry really took off. In 1862 there were 340 mines employing some 50,000 people, including boys as young as 12. Thousands of younger boys and women known as 'Bal Maidens' would earn a few coins breaking rocks on the surface and miners' wives are said to have invented the Cornish pastie as a satisfying, easily-handled meal for their menfolk. Some pasties had a mutton and vegetable filling in one half with a separate pastry pocket for pudding (usually stewed apple) in the other.

Life down a tin mine was hard and often fatal. Passages were cramped and unbearably hot – well over 50° – and so airless that candle flames became starved of oxygen. Access to deeper adits were via wooden ladders (no cages here to haul the workforce up and down) and roof falls or explosions were considered occupational hazards. Those who survived these daily perils would often suffer lung conditions such as consumption (TB) or bronchitis in later life. Rheumatism and arthritis were rife and it was rare to find a working miner in his forties.

For owners the hazards were all financial. Some tin mines, like Carn Galver on the St Ives – St Just road, were plagued by poor drainage and never became truly profitable. Others such as Giew Mine at Cripplesease were worked successfully for well over 150 years. Yet even a productive business could be threatened by world markets and in 1872, when huge ore finds were reported in New South Wales and Queensland, the Cornish industry was plunged into crisis. Further competition from Malaya and Bolivia meant that by the 1930s, barely half-a-century on from the boom years, it was virtually bust.

Throughout the rest of the 20th century there were occasional false dawns and whispers of a revival. But this was largely speculator talk and sadly on March 6th, 1998, the UK's last tin mine at South Crofty turned off its pumps, allowing water to flood the deeper passages.

Since then a campaign has been launched to preserve Cornwall's mining region as a World Heritage Site. Archaeologists have identified more than 2,000 mines and it seems the Age of the Tinners will soon be recognised as a milestone in the world's industrial past.

Opposite: *Abandoned tin-mine engine houses are a definitive feature of West Cornwall's magnificent coastline.*

MERRY MAIDENS AND STONED HURLERS

The hills around St Ives are a treasure trove of ancient history and folklore. Cultural motives for erecting the great Bronze Age stone circles and standing stones remain unclear although thousands of years later Puritan preachers adopted sinister explanations to ram the fear of God into their congregations.

The two likeliest examples of Christian spin-doctoring can be found in tales linked to the Merry Maidens circle, just off the Newlyn to Land's End road, and the Hurlers of St Cleer. Whatever the original purpose of these 4,000-year-old sites, it's feasible that they were used for Druid ceremonies around the time of Christ. They were certainly imbued with magical powers by country people, and to late Puritan England, obsessed as it was with witchcraft and the devil, they were ungodly places to be shunned by the faithful.

So we find that the Merry Maidens, the best-preserved circle in Cornwall, are actually the remains of 19 young women turned to stone as punishment for dancing on the Sabbath . A couple of musicians – who should obviously never have taken the gig – got the same treatment and can be found just to the northeast (they're known as The Pipers). Incidentally, don't be confused by references to the circle as Dawn's Men. This is a corruption of *Dans Maen*, Cornish for 'stone dance'.

A little way north at St Cleer, on the edge of Bodmin moor, an uncannily similar legend has it that a group of men were playing a Sunday hurling match when St Clarus, one of the early Christian missionaries, ordered them off to church. They refused and instantly got the full transmutation treatment. Since then the hurlers have got their own back by refusing to let themselves be counted. Only when a baker places penny loaves on each stone, and tallies up the bill, does the true number become clear. When you've stood in a lonely, damp Cornish field for centuries little victories like this really *matter*.

The clearest glimpse of Iron Age Cornwall, when sea-trade links between western Britain, Ireland, France and Spain were already established, emerges at Chysauster village south of St Ives near Penzance. Chysauster was occupied between the 1st century BC and 3rd century AD and comprises eight oval stone-walled homes, complete with terraced gardens, laid out in two rows along what is claimed to be Britain's first street. There is also a long underground passage, or fogou, a feature found only in Cornish Iron Age settlements, which was probably used either as a defensive refuge or for rituals. Chysauster's fogou has sadly collapsed but there's a great example just up the road at Carn Euny, near St Just.

Cornwall is synonymous with 'Celtic' identity, although in recent years the whole idea of 'Celticness' has become an archaeological hot potato. The idea that much of central and western Europe was once occupied by a single race of Ancient Celts is simply wrong and in fact the Cornish, Welsh, Scottish and Irish didn't start describing themselves as Celtic until the 18th century. However, there's no doubt that those nations – including Cornwall – do have a rich and definable culture which they're surely entitled to call Celtic if they wish. These days, they even risk a song and dance on Sundays.

Folklore, magic and religion come together in Cornwall's mysterious Bronze Age megaliths such as Lanyon Quoit, (opposite) *a neolithic burial chamber tomb and Men-an-Tol,* (below) *a cromlech – a Breton/Welsh word –* crom *meaning 'bent' and* llech *meaning 'flagstone'.*

WRECKERS, SMUGGLERS AND LADY PIRATES

The rugged coastline around St Ives has yielded more than mere fish to sustain the locals. Wrecking, salvaging, smuggling and piracy have all helped boost the economy over the years… to the consternation of the Revenue men.

You might think such questionable activities would be the exclusive preserve of horny-handed fishermen and village vagabonds. While they certainly had a slice of the action there were plenty of churchmen and bent government officers willing to hide the odd cask of looted brandy. One apocryphal story tells how a Cornish vicar was in the middle of his sermon when a breathless man dashed into church shouting 'Shipwreck!'. The vicar pleaded for his congregation to remain seated and locals feared he would waste time leading prayers for the drowned. No worries though. 'Let us tek aff us cassock,' said the vicar, 'so's us ken all start fair.' Then, cassock-less, he hot-footed it down the aisle.

Church tombs and family crypts were excellent hiding places for booty and the Reverend Richard Dodge, who became vicar of Talland, Cornwall, in 1713, was hand-in-glove with the local villainry. He spread rumours that his churchyard was bedevilled by ghosts and it was said he could summon evil spirits at will. The 'Preventive Men' avoided his church whenever possible.

By the end of the 18th century St Ives was a black marketeer's paradise. The village's official Collector of Customs between 1762 and 1782 was Sir John Knill, who used his position as perfect cover for illegally trading wrecked goods. So grateful was he for local support that he ploughed some profits into raising a 15

m (50 ft) high obelisk on a hill above the village. He also bequeathed money for a five-yearly ceremony (next due in 2011) in which ten maids dressed in white, accompanied by a fiddle player, lead the St Ives mayor, a vicar and a Customs officer on a procession around the obelisk singing the 100th Psalm 'All People That On Earth Do Dwell'. The event ends with refreshments in a local hostelry.

The gentry's habit of taking the government shilling while simultaneously doing business with crooks is long established in West Cornwall. The most deliciously ironic example involves Vice-Admiral Sir Henry Killigrew who in the 16th century was tasked with ridding the South-West Approaches of pirates (even though many of them were his pals). In fact, Sir Henry's wife, Lady Killigrew, dabbled in a little piracy herself while he was off patrolling, leading her household staff to ransack and steal a German merchant ship. She was later tried at Launceston Assizes but acquitted after Sir Henry bribed the jury.

It's sometimes easy to confuse the dreadful business of wrecking – in which ships were lured onto rocks by false lights – with salvaging, in which local people simply made the most out of washed-up cargo. As long as salvaged goods were declared to the Receiver of Wreck, no crime had been committed. This still holds true today; many of the so-called 'looters' who in early 2007 salvaged cargo from the MSC *Napoli* in Branscombe Bay, Devon, committed no offence.

St Ives has had plenty of 'useful' wrecks – the *Bessemer City* for example provided the village with months of tinned food when she went down off Clodgy Point in 1936. But the great prize for wreck-hunters is the mail packet ship *Hanover,* which foundered in 1763 off nearby Hanover Cove. This is now a protected site, probably just as well given that gold worth £50 million at today's prices was in the ship's hold.

Opposite and above: *The rugged west Cornwall coast has been a ships' graveyard for centuries. Salvage seekers once played a crucial role in the St Ives' economy.*

CLASSICAL SCANDAL

They were two of the greatest literary figures of the 20ᵗʰ century. Both spent a life-changing period close to St Ives – he in a hideaway cottage; she in an idyllic childhood holiday retreat. For D. H. Lawrence and Virginia Woolf, West Cornwall would offer fleeting moments of peace in lives racked by sadness, scandal and illness.

In Lawrence's case those moments were fleeting indeed. He'd returned to England with his German wife Frieda just as World War I broke out. British intelligence suspected her of being a German spy and by March 1916 the couple were renting a cottage at Zennor, west of St Ives, supposedly to escape the gossips and find solitude. In fact Lawrence almost immediately persuaded his friend, the publisher John Middleton Murry, and Murry's girlfriend, Katherine Mansfield, to take a cottage next door. It was a foursome made in hell. The Lawrences squabbled incessantly, Mansfield craved a return to city life and the men fell out after Lawrence suggested a blood-brother pact.

Things calmed down when Murry and Mansfield packed their bags, and for a time the 30-year-old Lawrence embraced his new Cornish lifestyle. He became friendly with some neighbours – the Hocking family of Tregerthen Farm – and there was much later speculation that Lawrence had a homosexual affair with William Henry Hocking. Frieda apparently suspected this and in the prologue to *Women in Love* Lawrence hints that he found William physically attractive.

By the autumn of 1916 local feeling had turned against the Lawrences. Many young Cornishmen were dying in the trenches so why wasn't he fighting for his country? (In fact Lawrence was twice rejected on health grounds). As for Frieda, she was obviously a spy. Locals accused her of showing lights to German submarines and hanging out her smalls according to a pre-arranged washing-line code. The Lawrences' cottage was searched by police and, although nothing was found, they were ordered out of Cornwall.

Lawrence would go on to write some of his greatest work, including *Women in Love* and *Lady Chatterley's Lover*, before his untimely death at 44. He refers to his Cornish sojourn in the 'Nightmare' chapter of *Kangaroo*.

Woolf's tragic life is well documented. She was sexually abused by her half-brothers, suffered a nervous breakdown at the age of 15, was institutionalised following the death of her father in 1904, and scandalised Twenties London during her lengthy lesbian affair with Vita Sackville-West. She took her own life in the most tragic of circumstances, weighing her pockets with stones and drowning herself. A last note to her husband, Leonard Woolf, includes the heart-rending line: 'Everything has gone from me but the certainty of your goodness. I can't go on spoiling your life any longer.'

Woolf's most vivid memories all stemmed from her family's holiday home, Talland House, which looks across Porthminster Bay, St Ives. Here she spent every summer until her mother's death in 1895 (when she was still only 13) writing, painting and walking. Throughout her life she was constantly drawn back to West Cornwall and she never forgot the stunning landscapes which would later drive her fiction. Her novel *To The Lighthouse* was inspired by the breathtaking view across the sand dunes of Hayle Towans out to the white, sentry-like tower of the Godrevy Lighthouse. If Virginia Woolf has a ghost, here's where you'll find her.

Opposite: *The Godrevy Light inspired Virginia Woolf's masterpiece* To The Lighthouse.

THE ST IVES ART COLONY

With its dramatic white façade curving gracefully above Porthmeor beach, Tate St Ives occupies arguably the most beautiful setting of any major art gallery in the world. It is a fitting monument to the St Ives School of painters who started the art colony here in rather more humble surroundings.

Like so many parts of Britain, St Ives was only 'discovered' by the Victorian masses with the opening of the railway. By the 1870s it was possible to make the entire journey from London by train and soon smitten tourists were telling friends about the town's quaint cobbled streets, whitewashed cottages and superb clutch of beaches washed by indigo seas. It was, they said, Cornwall's Bay of Naples.

The potential was not lost on the circle of wealthy, professional landscape artists who'd made their names at the Royal Academy. They arrived in St Ives just as West Cornwall's fishing and mining industries were in freefall with the result that studios, willing staff and suitably sea-weathered models were easy to find. Artists took over many of the old fishermen's lofts beside Porthmeor Beach, working alongside the locals and drinking in their pubs. They took on students, exhibited their work and became visitor attractions in their own right. Soon the 'St Ives School' had a worldwide reputation for maritime art.

World War I took its toll on the colony, wiping out an entire generation of young artists, but the arrival of studio potters Bernard Leach and Shoji Hamada in the 1920s

helped restore its fortunes. Key to this process was the painter Borlase Smart (1881–1947) who helped form the St Ives Society of Artists and encouraged the big London railway companies to commission the distinctive posters advertising the town as a holiday resort.

Over the next 40 years some of the greatest names in British art lived and worked in St Ives. The sculptor Barbara Hepworth and her husband Ben Nicholson were followed by the likes of Terry Frost, Patrick Heron and Bernard Leach. But by the 1960s landscape painting was becoming less fashionable. The London and New York 'pop art' phenomenon, with Andy Warhol as high priest, began to dominate and the St Ives School seemed doomed. The Porthmeor lofts, once buzzing with creativity, gradually decayed into weatherworn shells, ignored by the hordes of summer visitors as they streamed past en route to the squeaky-clean temple of the Tate. It seemed a sad, undignified end for a building of national cultural importance.

And yet, not quite the end. In 2006 the Borlase Smart-John Wells Trust, a charity dedicated to restoring Porthmeor as a working environment for artists, launched a £3 million appeal drawing on Arts Council and Heritage Lottery Fund grants. A few older fishermen still occupy some of the lofts – their equipment dating to the days before factory trawlers roamed the Atlantic – and hope one day to set up a permanent exhibition on their working lives. Equally important are the fortunes of some exciting artists now returning to Porthmeor and the town. The St Ives School isn't dead. Just sleeping.

Opposite: *The stunning main entrance at Tate St Ives.*
Below right: *Modern sculpture echoing the holed stones of prehistoric Cornwall.*

STAR GAZY FOR SUPPER

To its stream of summer visitors Mousehole is the archetypal Cornish fishing village, all lobster pots and slightly shabby fishing smacks. Beneath this cheerful face, though, lies a community with deep respect for the sea as giver, and taker, of life.

It's almost impossible to set foot in Mousehole – pronounced Mauzl – without becoming instantly assailed by images of Star Gazy pie. This curious concoction has whole pilchards, mackerel and sardines pushed heads up through the pie crust to give you an unnerving stare as you tuck in. You might think this is more than enough to handle over lunch but the Cornish, being Cornish, have made sure it comes with a hefty helping of sea yarn on the side.

The story goes that, many years ago, winter storms off Cornwall were so bad that the Mousehole fishing fleet couldn't leave harbour. For weeks people lived on the verge of starvation until finally, in a brief lull before Christmas, fisherman Tom Bawcock sailed bravely out to cast his nets. A pie of many fishes was made from the catch and Tom's feat is celebrated to this day on Tom Bawcock's Eve, December 23rd, when a Star Gazy feast is served up in the Ship Inn.

Sadly there's no evidence that Tom Bawcock ever actually existed. Bawcock is a Middle English word for a jolly good chap while Tom was once a generic name for adult males. Several fishermen may therefore have performed the heroic deed.

Over the years the festival has embraced a fantastic Christmas lights display in the harbour. However since December 19th, 1981 – the date of the Penlee lifeboat disaster – celebrations are briefly, poignantly, muted. Eight RNLI men, all from the Mousehole area, lost their lives that night and on the anniversary all illuminations apart from a single cross are switched off for an hour in their memory.

There's simply not enough space here to remotely do justice to the bravery of that lifeboat crew. If you read the transcript of radio exchanges, as recorded by the coastguard, you get some flavour of the calm, selfless way they laid down their lives. They were battling 15 m (50 ft) swells in 160 kmph (100 mph gusts) and at one point their boat, the *Solomon Browne*, was flipped on top of the stricken coaster *Union Star*. Unbelievably, they somehow got four people off the vessel – only to perish alongside them in the deadly, boiling waters.

The lifeboat from Sennen Cove tried go their aid but it was impossible her to round Land's End. The lifeboat of St Mary's, Isles of Scilly, joined in the search for survivors, and the lifeboat of the Lizard crossed Mount's Bay in hurricane conditions.

For the crew's friends and families, anxiously listening at home on radio scanners, hope gradually faded into despair. The only voices heard were the regular, haunting calls of the coastguard and circling Royal Navy Sea King helicopter pilot, punctuated by fishermen friends of the lifeboat coxswain Trevelyan Richards…

'Penlee Lifeboat from Falmouth coastguard, over…
'Penlee Lifeboat. Rescue Eight Zero. If you read me fire one flare….if you read me fire a flare….
'Can you hear us Trev…
'What is your position? Do you need any help? Shall we come out Trev…'

Both vessels were lost with all hands.

Next time you're in Mauzl, enjoy the charm, the warmth and the welcome of the locals. Have a bite of Star Gazy by the fire. And, maybe, pop a pound in the RNLI collection box.

Opposite: *On a balmy summer day Mousehole is a picture-perfect is a haven of peace.*

LAKE DISTRICT

Presented By Sally Whittaker

The *Coronation Street* star charts the development of the Lakes from one of a dark, foreboding landscape of previous centuries, to the tourist paradise of tranquility we see today.

EMERALDS AND SAPPHIRES

Every year millions of visitors flock to the Lake District to roam among its rich emerald hills and chill sapphire lakes. No matter if grey skies sometimes blend with slate, scree and drystone walls, nature's artbox remains the superlative reward.

Yet the Lake District's splendid desolation was not always appreciated by visitors. To Daniel Defoe, undergoing 'A Tour Thro' The Whole Island Of Great Britain' in the 1720s, the landscape of Westmorland proved 'the wildest, most barren and frightful of any that I have passed over in England'.

Nor was the arrival of trippers universally welcomed. Eminent Lakeland citizen poet William Wordsworth (1770–1850) wasn't pleased about the 'rash assault' on its 16 major lakes, concerned that the hordes had vulgar manners. He was sure that the poor and ill educated would not benefit 'mentally and morally', rather they would introduce 'wrestling matches, horse and boat races . . . pot houses and beer shops'. When he wrote a guide to the lakes in 1810 he recommended it only 'for the minds of persons of taste'.

This, of course, was even before the railways reached Westmorland, bringing with it many more trippers of all social shades. Drystone walls, a device to snatch land from the indigenous poor, were now admired rather than derided. The complexion of the place was undeniably changing.

Later it fell to children's author Beatrix Potter (1866–1943) to point up the audacity of visitors. Charabancs were too big for Lakeland roads, she maintained, and those who played music were especially despised. She was none too keen on visitors plunging into the cool waters of the lakes on hot summer days, either. 'Bathing is most perplexing. It seems cruel to refuse in hot weather but they should not do it at the exposed end of the lake.'

It may have been a nuisance to the great and the good who were resident in the region but tourism was undoubtedly a saving grace. As farmers' fortunes fell steadily in the last half of the 20th century, so tourism picked up the mantle for wealth creation in the region. At the moment about 12 million visitors come each year to soak up the landscape – and often the rain. Half of the 42,000 people who live in the National Park, established in 1951 to protect the area, make a living from tourism. On the other hand, just 10 per cent of the working population is involved in farming.

Books by Alfred Wainwright (1907–91) did much to beckon would-be walkers to the region. He was an office worker and hobby hiker who fell in love with the area after his first visit in 1930 but found existing guides inadequate. Initially written for his own edification, the popular guides took the mystery out of the crags and crevasses across the half million acres that make up the National Park.

And perhaps Wainwright is inadvertently to blame for one of the biggest dilemmas now facing park managers. The soil erosion caused by footfall on popular routes costs enormous sums to repair. Even the most conservation-conscious visitor cannot avoid destroying the special landscape merely by walking on it.

The ambience of the area remains, however, with each tarn and pike, every fell and force, a recognised gem in a national treasure.

Opposite: *All shades in nature's palette are reflected in Lakeland scenes like this one at Derwentwater.*

LAKE OF DESPAIR

An 8 km (5 mile) stretch of lake with glassy water fringed by forest and inlets, the atmosphere at Coniston is still and dolefully expectant. Perhaps it is the overpowering presence of Coniston Old Man, rising in the northwest to 802 m (2,631 ft), that renders it so.

It's not a peak in human form, of course, but a corruption of the Norse word for high, alt, while 'man' is local lingo for a summit. The slopes were once quarried, and industrial debris lying by landscape scars are reminders of the copper mining that once prevailed and the toil of long-dead miners.

The melancholy air doesn't emanate from the hills but from the water itself. It went from tranquil beauty spot to watery grave one day in 1967 when a British hero died trying to smash a water speed record. Sir Donald Campbell (1921–1967) had already set four of the seven records under his belt at Coniston. Another had been established at nearby Ullswater.

He was the son of a famous speed merchant Sir Malcolm Campbell (1885–1948) and grew up basking in the reflected glory of his father's triumphs. Ambitions to enter the Royal Air Force during World War II were thwarted by the detectable effects of childhood illness, leaving the younger Campbell anxious to prove himself on several counts.

When he took to the lake on the day of his death he was hoping to attract sponsorship for another record-breaking venture. The attempt began well and he achieved one dash across the lake at 478 kmph (297 mph) in his famous boat *Bluebird* without a hitch, already beating his personal record set three years previously in Australia. But on the return leg he cranked up the acceleration once more. Some estimates reckon he was travelling at more than 515 kmph (320 mph) when *Bluebird* suddenly reared up and flipped over backwards. Boat and pilot went to the 55 m (180 ft) depths of the lake.

There was little wreckage floating on the water, save for a soggy and misshapen teddy bear mascot known affectionately as Mr Whoppit. It was the toy that had accompanied Sir Malcolm on his ambitious jaunts and would later be taken into action by Sir Donald's record-breaking daughter Gina.

It was only in 2001 that body and boat were finally recovered. Sir Donald was laid to rest in Coniston cemetery where his headstone, engraved with bluebirds, gives testimony to his heroism.

Bizarrely his was not the only body in the lake. In 1976 mother of three Carol Ann Price, 30, disappeared from her home in Barrow, Cumbria, and it was assumed she had begun a new life elsewhere. However, amateur divers discovered her body 21 years later, bound and weighted on Coniston's floor, still wearing a baby doll nightdress.

Husband Gordon was arrested although initially charges against him were dropped through lack of evidence. But seven years later a jury decided the retired teacher had attacked his wife with an ice pick and sunk her body in the lake. Although he denied the charge he was jailed for life.

If there's a forlorn feeling to Coniston it's perhaps due to the ripples that continue today after the traumas that occurred there.

Opposite: *Coniston Water.*
Above: *In 1967 Coniston Lake was the destination of ill-fated record breaker Sir Donald Campbell, chosen for its generous length rather than its spectacular views.*

LOVING THE LAKES

For artists the chunky nugget of Derwenwater is the favoured lake, with light reflecting from its steep sides forever acclaimed and changing.

One of the artists most closely associated with the lake is the beloved children's author and illustrator Beatrix Potter. She spent happy family holidays at Derwentwater between 1885 and 1891, exploring its shoreline and sketching its abundant wildlife including red squirrels and hedgehogs. Her mind was all the time turning over storylines that emerged much later. Already in her twenties she was more concerned with her twin passions for drawing and animals than she was with romantic liaisons or a love life.

At the end of every summer Beatrix regretfully returned to her home in London. Only after she became a published author in 1902 with *The Tale of Peter Rabbit* could she at last fulfil her dream of having a home in her beloved Lake District.

In 1905 she bought Hill Top, a small working farm in Sawrey that's now a place of pilgrimage for Potter fans from all over the globe. This was the backdrop for many of her tales, and it was here that the 39-year-old Beatrix fled to grieve when her fiancé suddenly died, although her first home remained London where she cared for her ageing parents.

Only when she married a local solicitor at the age of 47 did she live full time in the area, having bought a nearby farm where she worked anonymously among her beloved Herdwick sheep. When she died she instructed that Hill Top remained untouched and its authenticity is a large part of its charm.

While the name Potter is synonymous with the Lake District, that of Hardwicke Drummond Rawnsley

(1851–1920) is not. Yet without this clergyman Potter might have remained unpublished and it was he who created the National Trust to protect vulnerable countryside, keeping the Lake District special.

He first met Beatrix when her family holidayed at Wray Castle, one of the Victorian excesses that stud the banks of Windermere. They struck up an enduring friendship and he eventually encouraged her to submit work for publication.

Already he had started the Lake District Defence Society, convinced that progress would bring ruination to the area. In 1893 he was the driving force behind the formation of the National Trust, with Potter's father Rupert one of the earliest life members. Between 1902 and 1908 the Trust gained much of the land around Derwentwater and Borrowdale. Eventually he became Canon of Carlisle Cathedral and was also the co-founder of a School of Industrial Arts in Keswick.

Another unknown who changed the face of Derwentwater was Joseph Pocklington, a wealthy Nottinghamshire banker who set his sights on Derwent Island in 1778. Once the home of 16th century German miners he transformed it with a Palladian villa and indulged in various follies including a church – unconsecrated and used to store beer – and six-gun batteries which fired at an 'armada' during regattas.

A charitable man, he earned the affection of local people who called him 'King Pocky' although he was derided by the literary community. He also bought the Bowder Stone in Borrowdale, a natural wonder weighing 1,870 tons. By it he built a chapel and a cottage to house a Bowder Stone guide. In 1807, visiting poet Robert Southey (1774–1843) called it 'hideous' meddling, 'for the place is as beautiful as eyes can behold or imagination conceive'. However, as another of Pocklington's Derwentwater homes, Barrow House, is now the youth hostel so his contribution to lakeland life may yet be more durable than that of Southey's.

Opposite: *Derwentwater, once the annual holiday destination for children's author Beatrix Potter.*
Above right: *Potter's Lake District home.*

WATER, WATER EVERYWHERE

Windermere is the Lakeland junction to which all travellers are drawn. At 17 km (10½ miles) in length and at times a 1½ km (1 mile) wide it exceeds the dimensions of its neighbours by some margin.

Given the traffic both on the water and on the road that runs its length, the throb of speedboat engines and the hum of cars frequently fills the air. The towns on its banks, Ambleside and Bowness, also groan with crowds. But Windermere is large and its shoreline ample so tranquillity is never far away.

Sometimes the lake is larger than ever. Heavy rains in January 2005 raised Windermere's level by a metre, which equates to a staggering 17,000,000,000 litres (3,740,000,000 gal) of water.

And it is the region's abundance of water that attracted the attention of Manchester Corporation when it was struggling to provide it in the rest of the northwest. Its factories were thirsty and its population would be too if supplies were not substantially enlarged. As a consequence, two Lakeland valleys are now underwater having been turned into reservoirs.

Thirlmere was created in 1894 at the cost of Armboth and Wythburn despite an orchestrated campaign to save the settlements. In 1935 Mardale and Measdale were drowned when the length of Haweswater was doubled. To do so engineers built a 470 m (1,410 ft) dam standing some 27 m (81 ft) tall that was an engineering triumph. It created a reservoir holding 84.5 billion litres (18.6 billion

gal) of water, an amount sufficient for everyone on the planet to enjoy three baths.

Conservationists mourned the loss of the landscape that, during dry spells, is tantalisingly exposed once more. Alfred Wainwright said: 'If we can accept as absolutely necessary the conversion of Haweswater [to a reservoir], then it must be conceded that Manchester have done the job as unobtrusively as possible. Mardale is still a noble valley. But man works with such clumsy hands! Gone for ever are the quiet wooded bays and shingly shores that nature had fashioned so sweetly in the Haweswater of old; how aggressively ugly is the tidemark of the new Haweswater!'

Yet nature has responded well to man's meddling, the awkward lines of pines have mellowed and Haweswater is rich in wildlife and two golden eagles, England's only pair, took up residence nearby.

But back to busy Windermere where one oasis of calm is currently out of bounds to the public. Privately owned Belle Isle is worthy of note for its astonishing Georgian round house and for speculation rife at the end of the 18th century that it was the bolt-hole for a notorious villain.

Fletcher Christian had organised the infamous mutiny on HMS *Bounty* in 1789. While Captain Bligh faced a perilous journey to safety in an open boat Christian headed for Tahiti. Despite global searches he was never found and fellow mutineers refused to betray his whereabouts. Meanwhile, the mile-long Great Island, as it was then known, was bought by his cousin Isabella Curwen. Could the hunted Christian have found his way to Windermere and hidden on the tree-lined isle? There was even talk that he was buried there. No grave has ever been found although it is known that Belle Island was named for the glamorous Isabella and that her descendants lived there until 1993.

Opposite and above left: *Lake Windermere attracts large crowds yet isolation is never far away, especially for the fortunate few who visit privately owned Windermere Island.* **Above right:** *The tranquility of the region is such that England's only pair of Golden Eagles took up residence close by and continue to thrive.*

OF KINGS AND VIKINGS

The crystal waters of Ullswater, the crisp air above Wastwater and the rocky ridges of Helvellyn are all part of a Lakeland story that continues to evolve.

However, events of the distant past are still wreathed in mountain mists. It's thought that the Rheged – a native people who probably co-existed with the Romans – once ruled in Cumbria. One early king, Coen Hen, is said to be the inspiration for *Old King Cole*. At the time the word for brothers was 'cymbrogi' and that's how that name Cumbria came about.

By the 7th century the Angles had arrived. Legend has it that the last king of Cumbria was Dunmail. He was slaughtered in a battle that took place between Grasmere and Keswick between his army and the combined might of Edmund I of England and Malcolm I of Scotland in 945. His captured sons had their eyes put out by the victors while his body was hauled to the ridge overlooking Grasmere and buried under a pile of boulders, a point known today as Dunmail's Raise.

The stragglers that survived snatched Dunmail's crown and cast it into Grisedale Tarn, with the words: 'Till Dunmail come again to lead us.' Every year warrior ghosts return to the tarn, retrieve the crown, and carry it down to the cairn on Dunmail Raise. They hit their spears on the top of the cairn, only to hear a voice saying 'Not yet, not yet; wait awhile my warriors.'

It's a fine tale, not unlike that of King Arthur whose father, Uther Pendragon, is sometimes linked with the region. Uther has been described in texts as a Lakeland dragon slayer as well as a giant.

But there's little certainty attached to any aspect of the tale. Dunmail might have been British or a Norseman. The date of the battle is confirmed in several old texts but some hold that Dunmail – if that was his name – survived to die later in Rome.

If he was king of Cumbria then it's highly unlikely that his realm followed the (controversial) lines of today's county boundary. It may well have included distant Strathclyde, as per ancient manuscripts – or that could be an alternative name for the region. We do know that the place was overwhelmed with Norse influences. Windermere has a Norse name translating to 'Vinandr's Lake' while counting at sheep auctions, even today – yan, tan, tether, mether, pimp – is done in the language of the Norwegian settlers some 1,300 years ago. Words commonly found in Cumbria including thwaite, gill and fell were all introduced by the Danes, as were Herdwick sheep.

It seems likely that conquering Normans encountered some resistance in the region or at least they made little headway by the time the *Domesday Book* was compiled in 1086. Only marginal amounts of the area were noted in the records. By this time the Scots who ruled after Dunmail had been ousted by Anglo Saxons from Northumberland. In 1092, however, William II decided to make the region his own.

Afterwards, sites around the lakes were continually caught up in the border wars between Scotland and England. However, it wasn't for the glorious vistas that various invaders came but for rich mineral deposits including lead, copper, zinc, graphite and coal.

Opposite: *The glorious waters of Ullswater viewed from Pooley Bridge.*

A POET'S PLAYGROUND

*'I wandered lonely as a cloud
That floats on high o'er vales and hills,
When all at once I saw a crowd,*

*A host, of golden daffodils,
Beside the lake, beneath the trees
Fluttering and dancing in the breeze.'*

Perhaps the most oft-quoted poem in Britain, the words of William Wordsworth's *Daffodils* are an affectionate tribute to the lakes he loved.

Wordsworth was born in Cockermouth, a fishing port on the Cumbrian coast. By the time he was a teenager both his parents were dead and he was separated from his siblings after being sent to Hawkshead Grammar School. Aspirations to join the clergy vanished after he went to Cambridge University where studies came a poor second to social events. During a European holiday in which he fathered a child following a love affair, he admitted he wanted to be a poet, high ambition for someone of limited means.

In the company of sister Dorothy – no mean wordsmith herself – he stayed with fellow writer Samuel Taylor Coleridge (1772–1834) in Somerset and the pair struck up a fruitful working relationship. Together they produced *Lyrical Ballads* published in 1789 which ushered in a new literary Romantic Age.

It wasn't until 1799 that William and Dorothy moved to Dove Cottage, Grasmere, in pursuit of an inspirational environment – and found the Lakes fitted the bill. The *Daffoldils* poem appeared for the first time in 1807 in *Poems in Two Volumes*. It typifies the simple and evocative language he chose above more obscure wordplay that was previously popular. The daffodils in question were at Gowbarrow Park on the banks of Ullswater and the work is a celebration of spring.

In 1802 he married Mary Hutchinson and fathered five children with her. As they still lived with Dorothy, Mary's sister Sarah and assorted visiting literary figures they needed more room and moved to Rydal Mount, some 3 km (2 miles) distant.

Thereafter his life was chequered. Although his fortunes increased with the popularity of his poems he fell out with Coleridge. His brother John died and his adored sister Dorothy was invalided with illness. Two children, Catherine and Thomas, died in childhood in 1812. The majority of the 70,000 lines of verse he produced had already been written.

The greatest accolade he received was to be made Poet Laureate in 1843 upon the death of neighbour and friend Robert Southey, an honour he held for seven years until he died, in 1870, of a lung infection. His grave in St Oswald's Church, Grasmere, is marked by a simple headstone.

Wordsworth, Coleridge and Southey are all closely linked to the Lakes, as is John Ruskin (1819–1900) who bought a house, Brantwood, above Coniston in 1871. Here he retreated after a series of mental breakdowns although he still found the wherewithall to make a name as one of the first 'green' campaigners

Later still Arthur Ransome (1884–1967), who had been to school at Windermere, settled in the Lake District after a globe-trotting career as a journalist with his wife Evgenia Petrovna Shelepina – once a secretary to Russian revolutionary Leon Trotsky. He wrote a dozen children's adventures, notably *Swallows and Amazons*, inspired by the Lakes but not specific to them. The sentiments of the luminous literary figures who found revelations among the peaks and fells can be summed up in a line borrowed from Wordsworth. It was, he said 'the loveliest spot that man hath ever found'.

Opposite: *The beautiful Rydal Mount, where poet William Wordsworth made his family home.*

NORTHUMBRIAN COAST

Presented by

Janet Street-Porter

Taking in the legend of King Arthur,
the beauty of Lindisfarne Island,
the impregnability of Bamburgh
Castle and of course the
landscapes that have made the
Harry Potter films such a hit,
Janet Street-Porter marvels at
the variety of views on offer.

BAMBURGH BESIEGED

By the mid-15th century the Wars of the Roses were tearing England apart. The rival royal dynasties of Lancaster and York fought almost incessantly and the ruling Lancastrian monarch, the weak and mentally unstable Henry VI, was eventually cornered at Bamburgh Castle. From here his wife, Margaret of Anjou, hatched a desperate plan to revive his fortunes.

In 1464 Henry and Margaret had been pursued to Bamburgh by the Earl of Warwick, who at the time backed the Yorkist king Edward IV. The Earl surrounded the castle but the couple escaped and Margaret later reached the safety of Berwick on a fishing smack. Bamburgh's defenders held out for a while but after slaughtering and eating their horses they chose surrender over starvation.

Within four months Henry and Margaret had re-possessed the castle and began a counterattack on Warwick. The Queen, who by now was effectively running the Lancastrian show, hoped to build a mini-kingdom defended by Bamburgh and the neighbouring fortresses of Alnwick and Dunstanburgh. But she was again repulsed and set sail for France seeking allies to help her defeat the Yorkist 'usurper' Edward. This time, however, she left Henry behind and there seems little doubt that Warwick could have taken the castle. Yet by now he had a private agenda and may have been preparing to switch sides.

For a while Edward put up with Henry's irritating presence at Bamburgh. However, when spies reported persistent efforts by Margaret to rally her allies – she was, after all, niece of the French King, Charles VII – he decided enough was enough. He ordered Warwick to retake the castle by any means and deployed devastating new artillery, the great cannons named London, Dijon and Newe-Castel, as the besieging army's trump card.

Contemporary accounts show that Edward was less than pleased about the prospect of damaging Bamburgh, which he saw as his own property. He dispatched heralds warning the Constable, Sir Ralph Grey, not to make him bombard the castle… 'the which the King, our most sovereign lord, hath so greatly in favour seeing it marcheth so nigh his ancient enemies of Scotland, he especially desireth to have it whole, unbroken with ordnance. If ye suffer one great gun laid into the wall and be shot and prejudice the wall, it shall cost you the chieftain's head and so proceeding for every gun shot to the last head of any person within the place.' Put more succinctly, the defenders were being threatened with a beheading for every cannonball fired.

After a brief but effective bombardment – the first time artillery was used against an English castle – Sir Ralph capitulated and was later executed at Doncaster. Henry VI continued the defence of his crown, and was even briefly reinstated, but his life ended violently in the Tower of London in May 1471. The Yorkists would rule Britain for a further 14 years until the arrival on the throne of the Lancastrian Henry Tudor (Henry VII) in 1485.

Bamburgh Castle earns only a passing reference in the history books; a powerful fortress for a powerless monarch. As you look out across the long sea wall you can imagine the proud Queen Margaret, cloaked against the cold, setting sail for France. And Henry, trapped in his little kingdom, awaiting help which never came.

Opposite: *Bamburgh Castle ranks among northern Europe's most formidable ancient strongholds.*

DARLING OF THE VICTORIANS

'T'was on the Longstone lighthouse. There dwelt an English maid. Pure as the air around her. Of danger ne'er afraid. One morning just at daybreak. A storm toss'd wreck she spied. And tho' to try seemed madness. "I'll save the crew!" she cried.'

(The Grace Darling Song)

The story of Grace Darling, the lighthouse-keeper's daughter who helped row nine shipwreck survivors to safety off the Farne Islands, obsessed Victorian society for decades. Her immense courage in unforgiving seas is beyond question and she was rightly feted as a real-life heroine. But, over time, celebrity status became overwhelming. An entire 'Grace industry', fuelled by imaginative journalists and rapacious fans, left her bewildered and longing for peace.

The defining moment in her life came at dawn on September 7th, 1838. Grace and her father William awoke to see the SS *Forfarshire* aground on the Big Harcar, a treacherous reef over a kilometre (some 1,200 yards) from the islands' Longstone Lighthouse, which the family manned. With the Darlings' sons away, and no chance of a lifeboat launch from the mainland, 22-year-old Grace joined her father in their rowing boat to save the nine survivors of the 63 passengers and crew, who were desperately clinging to rocks.

Their plan was for William to shoulder the bulk of the rowing with Grace taking over as they neared Big Harcar. While he leapt onto the rocks to brief the survivors, she hove to, skilfully keeping the boat clear of danger. All nine were taken safely back to the lighthouse where the

Darlings nursed them for three days until a weather window allowed passage back to the mainland.

Over the next few days local, then national, newspapers picked up the story and Grace was propelled into a world she barely knew existed. She was portrayed almost as a living saint; a demure, dutiful daughter quietly content with her humble housekeeping role yet brave and resourceful when confronted with crisis. This was great stuff for Victorian politicians, preachers and columnists who loved nothing better than a role model with which to beat the Great Unwashed public. Two months after the rescue the Queen herself wrote praising Grace's selfless act and enclosing a reward of £50.

By now the world and his dog were after a piece of the Grace Darling phenomenon. Sketches of her rowing to the rescue, long hair trailing in the storm, appeared on plates, postcards, comic books, biscuit tins, cheap trinkets, pottery, trays – in fact just about anything that could be sold into an insatiable market. Fans wrote demanding locks of hair, portrait painters – the Victorian

equivalent of today's paparazzi – swamped her with requests for sittings and even William Wordsworth weighed in with some suitably romantic verse. When a highly fictionalised account of the rescue entitled *Grace Darling Or The Maid Of The Isles*, by Jerrold Vernon, appeared in 1839 it was seized upon by other authors and treated as fact.

Grace certainly made money out of her bravery but she wanted nothing of a celebrity lifestyle. 'I have seven apartments in the house to keep in a state fit to be inspected everyday by Gentlemen,' she coldly informed one correspondent who enquired whether she might like to travel more. Sadly she died just four years after the *Forfarshire* rescue, a victim of tuberculosis. She is buried at St Aidan's churchyard, Bamburgh.

Opposite: *Grace Darling fulfilled the Victorian ideal of a heroine but shunned celebrity status.*
Above: *Grace Darling's monument at St Aidan's churchyard in Bamburgh.*

HOGWARTS AND HARRY HOTSPUR

To a generation of Harry Potter film fans its Gothic walls and turrets are the definitive image of Hogwarts as seen during some breathtaking Quidditch tussles in *The Philosopher's Stone*. But in real life this is Alnwick Castle, Northumbria, one of England's greatest fortresses and home to another Harry who also started young in the hero business.

This was the amazing Harry 'Hotspur' Percy, one of the most colourful characters of medieval England. He earned his nickname through fearlessness, skilled swordsmanship and an adrenaline-fuelled desire to chase down his foes no matter what the odds. Sent into battle at the age of eight, and knighted at 11, he was only truly happy in a fight.

Born at Alnwick in 1364 his family traced their lineage direct to the Norman barons of William the Conqueror. The Percys were effectively the kings of northeast England and spent much of their time defending the patch from marauding Scottish earls during an interminable series of border disputes. It was in just one of these engagements – the 1388 Battle of Otterburn – that headstrong Harry killed the Scots leader, the Earl of Douglas, in hand-to-hand combat before heading off in pursuit of his routed troops. Unfortunately they were not quite as routed as Harry believed and he suffered the humiliation of being captured and ransomed back to his father, the Earl of Northumberland.

The Earl was a key powerbroker in English politics – he was married to Edward III's grand-daughter – and he played a major role in de-stabilising Richard II. He also smoothed the way for Henry IV to succeed the throne in 1399 though their relationship fell apart after Henry put Harry Hotspur in charge of subduing rebellions in North Wales. The King presumably took the view that as long as Harry was busy fighting someone, anyone, he couldn't possibly be making mischief. However when Henry refused to bankroll his young commander's campaign costs, Harry Hotspur became disenchanted.

Things went downhill fast in 1402 following the Battle of Homildon Hill (backdrop to the opening of Shakespeare's *Henry IV*). Hotspur had performed magnificently for the King during this Scottish campaign and had captured five earls. He believed their ransom would settle a large chunk of his unpaid overheads but the King was also broke and purloined the prisoners himself. It was the final straw and Hotspur avowed revenge.

The following year he formed an alliance with the Scots and the Welsh rebel Owain Glyndwr, marching against Henry at the Battle of Shrewsbury. But this proved a fight too far; his Welsh forces never arrived, he was outnumbered three-to-two and his treasured, crescent-handled sword was left back at camp by servants. Harry died in combat, his beheaded, quartered body later displayed as a warning to traitors.

There is one bizarre footnote to his life. Almost five hundred years later, when the first football clubs were being formed, the Percys happened to have a family seat on London's Tottenham Marshes. The local club needed an inspirational name… and so Tottenham Hotspur FC was born.

Today Alnwick Castle is open to the public and its Poison Garden – the first in Britain – includes strychnine, hemlock and deadly nightshade. Poisoning was never Harry Hotspur's weapon of choice though in the case of King Henry he might have made an exception.

Opposite: *The stately and imposing Alnwick Castle.*

BAMBURGH CASTLE AND KING ARTHUR

From its dramatic coastal perch Bamburgh Castle frowns down on the Northumbrian coast as though daring a challenge from invaders. This place is enmeshed with Arthurian legend and became the powerbase of the first great English kingdom, Northumbria.

The collapse of Roman rule left the region ruled by a native British tribe, the Bryneich, and later a fierce bunch of piratical incomers, the Angles or 'English'. In the mid-6th century AD an English king, Ida the Flamebearer, won control and established his kingdom of Bernicia. In 547 AD he made Bamburgh – then known as Din Guayrdi – his royal palace.

Over the next 50 years Bernicia defeated both the surrounding British tribes and the neighbouring Angle stronghold of Deira (centred on the Yorkshire Wolds) establishing the powerful new realm of Northumbria. Ida's grandson, Aethelfrith the Artful, became its first ruler and named Bamburgh after his queen, Bebba (it was originally Bebba's Burgh). His family dynasty really began the continuous royal history of England and Northumbria survived as a proudly independent Anglo-Saxon kingdom right up until the Norman invasion.

The strength of Bamburgh's links to King Arthur carry all the usual health warnings. A great British warrior-king probably *did* exist in the 6th century AD although his adventures as told in the 15th-century work by Sir Thomas Malory, *Le Mort d'Arthur*, are self-evidently fictional adaptations of folk legends. Malory suggests that Bamburgh was the home of the bravest Knight of the Round Table, Sir Lancelot, who called it Joyous Guard. However Malory also qualifies this by identifying Alnwick as an equally plausible location.

According to legend, Lancelot challenged the evil owner of the enchanted castle, Sir Brian of the Isles, over his fondness for gaoling passing knights and planting gravestones outside to pretend they were dead. Lancelot routed Sir Brian and his henchmen using magical shields but in order to completely free the knights from the heinous spell he had to spend 40 consecutive nights within the castle walls. As Lancelot was forever trooping off on quests this proved tricky and the prisoners became understandably miffed.

In the end Lancelot crept through the castle chapel into a cave below where he defeated a terrifying monster and obtained keys to unlock the spell from a maiden clothed in copper. The gravestones then disappeared and the knights walked free. Later, after his affair with Arthur's queen Guinevere was laid bare, Lancelot saved her from being burnt at the stake and took refuge with her in Joyous Guard.

The best you can say about the legend's Bamburgh link is that there certainly was a castle here in Arthur's time. Since the Anglo-Saxons were the King's sworn enemies, it would also have been natural for Lancelot to attack it and drive out Ida and Aethelfrith (or their forbears). The name Din Guayrdi may well have become Dolorous Guard, or Joyous Guard, over the years and 'Sir Brian' sounds uncannily similar to the name of the Bryneich leader King Bran Hen the Old. The 'Isles' in his title may refer to the nearby Farne Isles.

Opposite: *Could the dramatic Bamburgh have been the home of Sir Lancelot in Arthurian legend?*

THE LINDISFARNE GOSPELS

Lindisfarne, now called Holy Island, became one of the great seats of Christian learning during the 7th century AD. Pilgrims travelled from across northern Europe to pray at the tomb of the miracle-worker St Cuthbert and the magnificent illuminated Latin manuscript known as the *Lindisfarne Gospels* was produced here in his honour.

The island's monastery was founded by an Irish-born monk from Iona, St Aidan, around AD 635. He came at the request of Oswald, the newly restored Christian King of Northumbria, and together they formed an evangelical double act, with Aidan preaching and Oswald acting as interpreter. Converting heathens can hardly have been the easiest of missions but as the son of King Aethelfrith (see *page 184*), Oswald had the right genes for a challenge.

St Aidan died in 651 AD and, according to the Lindisfarne monks, the moment was relayed by divine vision to a shepherd boy called Cuthbert as he tended his flock on the Scottish border. That year Cuthbert entered the monastery at Melrose where his leadership and general saintliness earned him the title 'Fire Of The North'. He became prior ten years later and went on to establish a monastery at Ripon before moving to Lindisfarne, where his powers as a healer apparently reached new heights.

For a while Cuthbert lived the life of a hermit on Inner Farne, where he built a cell and oratory. With only seals and sea-birds for company he devoted himself to studying wildlife, and his notes on the eider duck – sometimes known as Cuthbert or Cuddy ducks – have led some to claim that he was the world's first conservationist. He also gave his name to Cuddy's Beads, found on the shores of Lindisfarne. These are actually fossilised Crinoid sea creatures which (if you squint a bit) resemble the outline of the cross. They were once used as rosary beads.

Cuthbert became the fifth Bishop of Lindisfarne in 685 but died two years later. He was buried on the island and many pilgrims who crossed the causeway at low tide to enter his shrine claimed to have been healed by the

'Wonder Worker of England'. By the early 700s the monastery had become a treasure chest of religious art and scholarship and a monk called Eadfrith, or Eadfrid, compiled the *Lindisfarne Gospels* (of Matthew, Mark, Luke and John) using traditional Celtic calligraphy and artwork. The book was placed on Cuthbert's tomb in an elaborate metal case (sadly since lost) and an Anglo-Saxon translation was added around the 10th century AD by a monk called Bilfrith. This is now the earliest surviving Old English copy of the *Gospels*.

Long after his death, St Cuthbert's influence on the faithful was immense. In 875, with the threat of Viking raids on Northumbria (see *pages 188–9)* the Lindisfarne monks fled, taking the saint's coffin with them. In a Pythonesque saga, they lugged it around for seven years, including a brief 'tour' to Ireland. During a rough Irish Sea crossing the *Lindisfarne Gospels* were lost overboard but

St Cuthbert then appeared in a vision and told the monks precisely where it would wash up on the coast. Three days later they found the book, stained but intact. It is now held by the British Museum and chemical analysis of the paper suggests it has indeed been in contact with salt water at some point.

St Cuthbert was eventually buried at Durham Cathedral in 1104. Those performing the internment insisted his body had remained unchanged in the 417 years since his death. The same was apparently true of King Oswald's head, which had been placed with the corpse for safe keeping.

Opposite: *St Cuthbert was hailed as a miracle worker among Christianised Anglo-Saxons.*
Above: *Lindisfarne Abbey, once rich in religious art and scholarship.*

THE PLUNDER OF LINDISFARNE

In the 8th century AD the Vikings brought terror to the Northumbrian coast. It wasn't that they were necessarily braver or better warriors but their fast, manoeuvrable longboats ensured a crucial element of surprise. The English were outraged, perhaps forgetting that their own Anglo-Saxon forbears once inflicted similar carnage.

The first clear sign of trouble came early in the reign of the Wessex king Beorhtric (786–802). The *Anglo-Saxon Chronicle* notes that in 787: '…King Beorhtric took Edburga the daughter of Offa to wife. And in his days came first three ships of the Northmen from the land of robbers. The reve then rode thereto, and would drive them to the king's town; for he knew not what they were; and there was he slain. These were the first ships of the Danish men that sought the land of the English nation.'

These lines emphasise the bewilderment that must have engulfed English coastal kingdoms. The king's reeve (court official) mentioned above was Beaduheard who confidently assumed the Danish visitors were merchants. He was trying to steer them to Dorchester for bureaucratic formalities; they killed him in cold blood.

Within six years the Vikings, encouraged by stories of English monasteries laden with treasure, launched an attack that would shake the whole of Christendom: the plunder of Lindisfarne.

The *Chronicle* entry for 793 reads:

'This year came dreadful fore-warnings over the land of the Northumbrians, terrifying the people most woefully: these were immense sheets of light rushing through the air, and whirlwinds, wand fiery, dragons flying across the firmament. These tremendous tokens were soon followed by a great famine: and not long after, on the sixth day before the ides of January in the same year, the harrowing inroads of heathen men made lamentable havoc in the church of God in Holy-island, by rapine and slaughter.'

A later (and therefore not totally reliable) account attributed to the writer Simon of Durham tells how the Danes… 'laid everything waste with grevious plundering, trampled the holy places with polluted feet, dug up the altars and seized all the treasures of the holy church. They killed some of the brothers; some they took away with them in fetters; many they drove out, naked and loaded with insults and some they drowned in the sea.'

It is hard to overstate the effect of the Lindisfarne raid on the early Church. The Northumbrian cleric Alcuin, an adviser to the Frankish king Charlemagne, claimed it was divine retribution for the sins of the people. He used a biblical quote to back up this theory – '…out of the north an evil shall break forth upon all the inhabitants of the land (Jeremiah 1:14)' – and urged repentance and spiritual reform. 'It is some 350 years that we and our forefathers have inhabited this lovely land,' he wrote in one letter home, 'and never before in Britain has such a terror appeared as this we have suffered at the hands of the heathen. Nor was it thought possible that such an inroad from the sea could be made.'

Then, in more forthright terms: 'The pagans have contaminated God's shrines and spilt the blood of saints in the passage around the altar, they have laid waste the house of our consolation and in the temple of God they have trampled underfoot the bodies of the saints like shit in the streets.'

Little wonder that when a second wave of Viking attacks began in the late 9th century the monks of Lindisfarne headed for Ireland – taking the body of St Cuthbert with them.

Opposite: *Traditional 'boat houses' on Holy Island.*
Below: *The Holy Island coast near 16th century Lindisfarne Castle.*

LIVERPOOL

Presented by
Jamie Redknapp

Legend of the Kop, the football
star highlights the close relationship
the people have to the River Mersey,
as well as the historical impact of
commerce on the city itself, and
the part it played in the slave trade.

BOOM TOWN

One of England's most unpopular kings he may have been, but King John (1166–1216) was the first to spot potential in Liverpool, granting it elevated status with a charter in 1207.

At the time it was a fishing village with little to recommend it. True, St Patrick stopped there briefly en route to Ireland but by the 11th century it amounted to no more than a church, a tower and a handful of huts. Even with royal approval it struggled to make an impact. By 1272 the population was only 840.

Liverpool's desirable proximity to the Irish Sea and to the Atlantic was ultimately its salvation. By 1442 it had its own castle which was under siege during the English Civil War and during the invasion by William of Orange but has since vanished under the heavy weight of development.

During the middle of the 18th century, with a population of 18,000, Methodist preacher John Wesley (1703–1791) said it was 'one of the neatest, best built towns I have ever seen in England'.

All that was about to change, though, with the slave trade, emigration and the agricultural revolution which brought in battalions of the rural poor. Within a decade Liverpool's population had swelled to 76,000 and was still rising.

By 1901 the census revealed there were more than 700,000 living in the city, many in straightened circumstances. Between 1906 and 1911 militancy grew,

culminating in the 72-day transport strike that paralysed the docks, the railways and the trams. Two men died after police charged a strike meeting.

Destiny nearly paved a different path. Remarkably, Liverpool was almost a spa town after quarry workers discovered a spring in 1773, the qualities of which were lauded by a local surgeon, James Worthington, for 'loss of appetite, nervous disorders, lowness of spirit, headaches proceeding from crudities of the stomach, Ricketts and weak eyes.'

In 1894 when bodies were moved in St James Cemetery the corpse of Captain David Gwin, who died in 1813 aged 76, was found completely petrified and as hard as stone. It was believed that the spring ran in that direction, and that minerals in the water caused this astonishing result. But analysis in 1924 cast doubt over its health-giving properties and the spring fell into disuse.

Industrial unrest aside, shipping remained vital to Liverpool, and not just in terms of the trade it created. Sailors who ate lamb stew known as scouse lent the name to natives. Shipping disasters were keenly felt, like that of the *Titanic* in 1912, which had a number of Liverpudlians among the crew. (Liverpool company CW & FN Black provided the musicians and famously demanded payment from the dead men's families for 'Loss of uniform'.) On a smaller scale, the wreck of the paddle steamer *Ellan Vanin* in 1909 on the Mersey Bar with the loss of 15 passengers and 21 crew also cast a pall over the city. The drama of it was captured in subsequent folk songs. The age of shipping duly waned, however, and by 1985 Liverpool's population had dropped to 460,000. Now regeneration was the name of the game and the docks were its first target.

Above: *Ships and docks were key to the rising and ebbing fortunes of Liverpool as its population swelled to extraordinary proportions.*

APEX OF THE SLAVE TRIANGLE

An unsavoury slice of Liverpool's history is linked with the slave trade, as its ships carried half of the three million slaves ripped from their families to an unknown fate at the behest of British slavers.

Slavery was the unacceptable face of capitalism rife in the burgeoning city. From 1699 until the 1807 Parliamentary bill abolished the trade in slaves, Liverpool sent out more ships to transport human cargo in dire conditions than any other British sea port and probably accounted for three-quarters of slave ship movements throughout Europe.

As the abolitionist movement gained momentum, some Liverpool dignitaries were fighting hard and dirty to keep slave trading alive. The object of their fury was specifically local lawyer and MP William Roscoe (1753–1831), an ardent abolitionist despite the unpopularity it brought to his door. One prominent citizen declared he would 'with pleasure, feast on Mr Roscoe's heart' and would burn down the activist's house to halt the abolitionist cause.

One of 64 anti-abolitionist bills that came out of Liverpool prior to 1807 warned that ending slavery would result in 'the prejudice of the British manufacturers, must ruin the property of the English merchants in the West Indies, diminish the public revenue and impair the maritime strength of Great Britain.'

Fewer than a dozen slaves found their way to Liverpool during these dark days. Rather, Liverpool financed and grew fat on the ships that left the port for West Africa loaded with manufactured goods. These were exchanged for slaves who filled the holds before the ships set sail for the West Indies or North America in the perilous leg of the trip now known as the middle passage. After the sale of the slaves to sugar plantations, the ships returned to Liverpool weighed down with commodities.

The slave trade is still in the ears and eyes of its residents today. Penny Lane, made famous by the Beatles in a song of the same name, was named for slaver Sir James Penny, and it's only one of a number of street names commemorating prominent slave traders.

Indeed, it was anti-abolitionist Penny who shamefully assured doubters that those transported from West Africa in chains lived 'better than gentlemen do on shore'. In fact transported slaves existed in painfully cramped conditions, were subject to terrible diseases, lived on starvation rations and were cruelly abused by the ship's crew.

For the eagle-eyed there are still friezes on public buildings today that include depictions of black people, illustrating the well-founded notion that Liverpool was built on the revenue of slavers. In fact, it's only partly true. While the slave trade involved more than 120 ships out of Liverpool a year before ending and brought considerable fortunes to those who backed it, this figure remained a fraction of port activity at the time. England was getting increasingly industrialised and there were plenty of other home-grown options for export. The gap in the market was swiftly filled and Liverpool's fortunes continued to boom even after slavery was abolished. By 1912 no less than 15 per cent of the world's total shipping came from the city. Significantly, though, the last slave trader ship to leave Britain in July 1807 was the *Kitty's Amelia* out of Liverpool.

Opposite: *William Roscoe wrote poems condemning slavery when human trade was bringing millions into a few Liverpudlian pockets. Finally he helped to outlaw it in the House of Commons.*

GATEWAY TO EMIGRATION

For those seeking adventure, a new life or merely one square meal a day in the 19th century it was destination: Liverpool. From here the riches of America, the expanse of Canada and the warmth of Australia were a comparatively short hop away.

About nine million people emigrated out of Liverpool in the century after 1830. There were English people, often the rural poor or aspiring middle classes, and a sizeable number of Germans who found the route from Liverpool quicker and cheaper than those from native ports.

But the majority came from Ireland. After 1847 the country – still an English dominion – was paralysed by the potato famine. As crops failed, those working on the land starved. The disaster sparked a bulge in emigration, especially among those travelling in steerage. In 1850, an estimated four out of five emigrants were Irish peasants or labourers, among them Patrick Kennedy, great-grandfather of American president John F. Kennedy.

Before leaving, their experience of Liverpool was often coloured by the poor quality of its boarding houses. Unable to board their ships until the day before departure, many had to find a bed for a night or even a week beforehand. The gullible were lured to unsavoury accommodation by unscrupulous 'runners', fast-talking fraudsters who preyed on emigrants as they prepared for the momentous voyage. Runners might hold luggage hostage for high prices or force people to take squalid lodgings. Often they took the last money the near destitute travellers possessed.

Nonetheless, brightly coloured posters advertising passages on lines including Cunard, White Star, Inman, Guion and National Lines plastered the walls of the dock areas. Shipping offices were a-buzz with activity. Until 1860 the ship was likely to be an elegant sail-powered vessel that would cross the North Atlantic in 35 days. Those bound for Australia might spend up to 17 weeks aboard.

Steerage meant large below-deck dormitories with little light and poor ventilation. At first the mood might be brightened by fiddle playing and dancing among passengers. But if diseases such as typhoid took hold then many would perish and there was little to do but wait. By 1900 third-class cabins were incorporated into ships improving conditions considerably.

As a ship sailed the dockside would be alive with well-wishers waving hats and handkerchiefs as passengers aboard responded in kind. Once the ship had left the quayside its crew began the search for stowaways – and were rarely disappointed. Men, women and children secreted themselves in bedding, barrels and boxes hoping for a free trip. Frequently they gave themselves away with a yelp as sailors used a sharpened stick to prod well-used hiding places. Those found were swiftly dispatched back to shore by rowboat.

Ships also bore first and second class passengers although these were fewer in number. By the late 19th century the number of those heading overseas had dropped. A revival in the 20th century between the wars proved no more than a blip in a downward trend.

Still, the mark of the Irish remained in Liverpool as ceilis, Irish music and dance became woven into the city's culture as, for a while, did sectarian disputes between Catholics and Protestants around the city.

Opposite: *With their sights set on a new life overseas, families flooded into Liverpool – the primary English embarkation point for emigrants.*

LARGER THAN LIFE

Times were tough in Liverpool in the first half of the 20th century. There was widespread poverty, job shortages and ill-health among those confined to its insanitary back streets.

But at least the residents of Liverpool could count on support from one formidable woman. Battling Bessie Braddock (1899–1970) made the welfare of Liverpudlians paramount when she was one of the area's MPs for 24 years. She nailed her colours to the mast in 1945 when she was elected to parliament in a maiden speech which focused on Liverpool's 'bug-ridden, lice-ridden, rat-ridden lousy hell holes'.

Bessie was the daughter of activist Mary Bamber (1874–1938) and as a child accompanied her to political meetings, strikes and soup kitchens. 'I remember the faces of the unemployed when the soup ran out. I remember their dull eyes and their thin, blue lips. I remember blank,

hopeless stares, day after day, week after week, all through the hard winter of 1906–7, when I was seven years old. I saw the unemployed all over Liverpool,' Bessie later recalled.

When Mary died her coffin was draped with a red flag and was hoisted aloft by members of the International Brigade, veterans of the fight against fascism in Spain.

Fleetingly a communist, Bessie identified more strongly with the Labour party that finally mushroomed in support at the end of World War II. She campaigned for forgotten causes, including mental health and prisons in a hard-hitting way, gaining a reputation for uncompromising stridency that ruffled even fellow party members. In addition she became a figurehead in the drive for fashions for larger women, herself sporting vital statistics of 50-40-50. In 1968 she was the first woman to be awarded the honorary freedom of Liverpool.

At her funeral Labour leader Harold Wilson said she was 'born to fight and never flinched from the battle'. She was the charismatic champion, he said, of the poor, lonely, old, sick, homeless, exploited and the deprived.

Liverpool had developed a tradition for producing redoubtable crusaders, although few emerged from her working class background. Liberal prime minister and reformer William Ewart Gladstone (1809–1898) was born and schooled in Liverpool, although his parents were Scottish. Eventually he went to Eton and Oxford but he never forgot his links with the city and it was here in 1896 that he delivered his last significant speech, a denunciation of the Turkish slaughter of Armenians.

In 1882 Thomas Frederick Agnew encountered the work of a child cruelty prevention society in New York. The following year, after he returned to Liverpool, he began a similar society that eventually blossomed into the National Society for the Prevention of Cruelty to Children. Charles Booth (1840–1916), a prominent campaigner on behalf of the poor, was also a Liverpudlian.

Although not born in Liverpool, politician William Huskisson (1770–1830) did much to foster trade in the city and died at the opening of the Manchester to Liverpool railway, under the wheels of Stevenson's Rocket.

Other more surprising Liverpudlians include William Hitler, son of German dictator Adolph's half-brother Alois, *Titanic* survivor J. Bruce Ismay, of the White Star Line, and Jeremiah Horrocks (1618–1641), the man who first discovered Venus.

Opposite: *Liverpudlians at play still found something to smile about even though sorry living conditions.*
Right: *The city's ills and the plight of it's people were frequently publicised by Bessie Braddock.*

MUSIC AND MAYHEM

One super group put Liverpool indelibly on the musical map and it was, of course, The Beatles. However, John, Paul, George and Ringo did not pioneer the city's 'Mersey Beat' phenomenon, only the hysteria that surrounded it.

Before they had embarked on a blazing trail Billy Fury (1940–1983) had become the first Liverpudlian chart buster. After short-lived jobs as a welder and on dockland tugboats he was spotted at the Birkenhead Essoldo in 1958 and dispatched to stardom by impresario Larry Parnes. Fury even had the dubious honour of being one of the men to turn down The Beatles. When the group auditioned for the job of his backing band Fury thought bass player Stu Sutcliffe was under par. However, Lennon refused to ditch his pal.

The other man famously in the same camp was Dick Rowe from Decca Records who assured manager Brian Epstein: 'Guitar groups are on the way out.'

To put Fury and Rowe's blunder into perspective there was a glut of beat bands around Liverpool at the time. Nor was the Cavern Club, the place with the reputation for making The Beatles great, one of the few venues. One estimate put the number of groups as high as 300, performing in the city's 200 pubs, clubs and cellar bars at lunchtimes and evenings in the early Sixties.

Like the rest, The Beatles put in hard work for several years before achieving the number one spot in 1962 with *Please Please Me*. They performed in Germany in gruelling tours during which Stu Sutcliffe died of a brain haemorrhage. Drummer Pete Best was replaced by Ringo Starr – who was himself subbed on some early recordings. However, the ensuing Beatlemania distinguished them from the rest. Even today the Beatles – singly and together – draw fans to Liverpool.

In the wake of the Beatles came a host of successful singers and bands, trading on what was now a recognised Liverpool brand. Cilla Black, The Searchers, Freddie Starr and Billy J. Kramer were in the Mersey stable. Gerry and the Pacemakers exploited the tidal wave of Liverpudlian sentiment with *Ferry Cross the Mersey* and *You'll Never Walk Alone* which was number one for four weeks in 1963. Originally written for the Rogers and Hammerstein musical *Carousel* in 1945, it soon became adopted as the anthem for Liverpool Football Club and rings around the Anfield ground every home game.

Alongside the Mersey music came poetry proving the truth of Peter Ansorge's famous quote: 'Liverpool loves language – spoken or sung rather than written down – and for a time the whole country applauded.'

Ten years after Beatlemania Liverpool was once again at the heart of a music trend, this time Northern Soul. A new sound with its roots in the Merseybeat but a wholly different end product came to the fore in the 1970s inspired by The Real Thing, a chart-topping group that also had to wait patiently for the big time. For a while the Mardi Gras club became the epicentre of Northern Soul, the former cinema hosting gigs by Ben E. King and Al Green.

A decade later and a new nightclub was dominating. Eric's was described as 'the sort of place you could have a nervous breakdown and nobody would notice'. Punk and new wave acts played there and aspiring stars flocked to watch, including Holly Johnson who later helped to define the Eighties music scene in *Frankie Goes to Hollywood*.

Opposite: *John Lennon (1940–80), singer, songwriter and founder of The Beatles, was born in Liverpool and often performed in its clubs before making the big time.*

THREE GRACES

In Ancient Greece the Three Graces were the goddesses of splendour, festivity and rejoicing. Daughters of Zeus, the trio warmed men's hearts and bellies, offering a general sense of well-being to all those in their company.

Centuries later a trio of buildings standing sedate by the Mersey have been christened the Three Graces. The three are a comforting reminder of the commercial glories once associated with Liverpool, second city of the empire. As a familiar skyline they are a 'welcome home' sign to travellers. Liverpudlians are a sentimental bunch and, for reasons mostly associated with tradition, the Three Graces – symptomatic of all that's best about life in Liverpool – evoke a tide of emotions.

The buildings in question are the Royal Liver Building, built between 1908 and 1911 and topped by birds that look like prehistoric cormorants. One theory says the birds are eating lyver, or seaweed, and that's why they are now known as liver birds and have become symbols of the city.

Next door and in the middle of the three is the Cunard Building, completed in 1916 for the company that made fine ships. Although aeroplanes were flying at the time no one knew they would one day hijack world travel. Last in line is the Port of Liverpool Authority building, dating from 1907 and, like the other two, opulently appointed. Plans for a 'fourth grace', to mark this being the European Capital of Culture in 2008, are under consideration.

Liverpool has twice as many cathedrals as is normal in a city, both modern creations. The Catholic one is the Metropolitan Cathedral although it is better known as

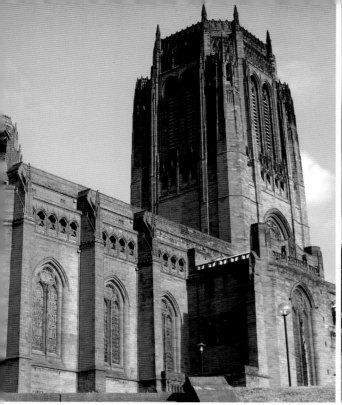

'Paddy's Wigwam' or the 'Mersey Funnel' finished in the 1960s. Nearby is the later – but taller – Anglican cathedral which boasts the world's tallest Gothic arches and the highest and heaviest bells.

A port is often peopled with men staring moodily out to sea. Some are keen to set sail for new shores while others are sorry to leave. To mark the mixed emotions raging beneath those calm faces and vacant eyes one artist studded a shoreline with a phalanx of such men. Antony Gormley used his own body as an inspiration for statues rooted along a three kilometre (2 mile) stretch of Crosby beach. He made 100 of them in cast iron and placed some a kilometre deep in estuary water. The sight of a man disappearing mutely beneath the waves had a disturbing effect not only on visitors but also on the local authority, anxious that this immobile army was a danger to small boats and ambitious swimmers.

Plans to rid the beach of the men caused uproar. Finally a compromise plan in which some were removed to safer locations saved the remarkable art installation for future generations.

Some things change and some stay the same, including the mindset of Liverpudlians. This quote came from a time when the foundations of the Port of Liverpool building were the only evidence of the Three Graces. Yet few would claim the spirit of the city now encapsulated by the waterfront edifices has changed.

'I have never seen any place like Liverpool. Liverpudlians are proud of their birth place, not only for its history, supremacy as a sea port, delightful situation and surroundings, but because of its preeminence of its merchant princes and citizens stability, integrity, progressiveness and humour'. (*Recollections of a Liverpudlian*, 1908)

Opposite: *Liverpool has an abundance of fine buildings, including the Three Graces on the waterfront that have now become a brick signature for the city and its residents.*
Above left and right: *There are two competing cathedrals to serve a diverse population.*

HADRIAN'S WALL

Presented by Clive Anderson

Trying to keep the Celts at bay
meant the Romans building and
manning for centuries one of
Britain's most iconic fortifications.
We delve into its history, as well
as detailing life for the ordinary
legionnaire in a hostile Britain.

SYMBOL OF POWER

When Hadrian succeeded his great uncle Trajan as Roman Emperor in 117 AD he knew the days of conquering vast swathes of Europe were over. The army had enough to do, particularly in the Empire's far northwest corner where British tribes were wreaking havoc.

Hadrian was an intelligent leader whose impressive memory, it is said, allowed him to name every officer in his legions. A decorated soldier with a strong grasp of battlefield strategy he also had a talent for art and design. Above all, he loved to build. Both the Pantheon and his Tivoli villa ranked among his most treasured achievements.

By the time he arrived in Britain (around AD 120) he'd already approved two new military frontiers: the River Euphrates in Asia and a wooden barrier in Germany. But his northern British wall, designed, in the words of his biographer, 'to divide the Romans from the barbarians', was by any measure a truly incredible engineering feat.

Hadrian's motive is debatable – and ego may well have been a factor – but the psychological impact of the wall on rebels must have been immense. It symbolised power, control, knowledge and discipline; the very attributes they lacked. In an era which restricted Hadrian's chances of campaign glory, it must also have played well with the senators back home.

The wall runs for almost 130 km (80 miles), from the outskirts of modern-day Newcastle in the east to the Solway Firth in the far west. It embraces the natural barrier of the River Tyne, the wild, rugged dolerite crags of the Whin Sill, the north side of the River Irthing valley and the Solway estuary. Best estimates suggest it took 10,000 men around ten years to build, during which time nearly four million tons of rock had to be quarried by hand and dragged by horse-drawn wagon into position. As an added defence a ditch up to 12 m (40 ft) wide was dug on the northern side.

The 72-km (45-mile) long eastern section was built entirely of stone while west of the Irthing crossing turf was originally the preferred material. It's not clear why this decision was made – perhaps the rebel threat was greater in the east – but supply lines and army manpower would have been a factor. What seems clear is that the 'milecastles' (mini-forts spaced at 1.6 km [1 mile] intervals) and lookout turrets (two between each milecastle) were built first with the wall filling inbetween. Milecastle gateways were built even when they opened onto a cliff face, suggesting a slavish obedience to Rome's military bureaucrats.

There are many tantalising mysteries surrounding the wall's practical uses but perhaps the greatest is… what was it *for*? Some historians argue that Hadrian simply wanted to control north-south trade and movement. Others believe it would have deterred raids on farms and livestock (getting through the wall was one thing; driving large flocks back under pursuit quite another). But the structure's dimensions are bizarrely grandiose if these were the main motives. Besides, the legions reigned supreme as offensive units strategically superior in an open battlefield. Defending entrenched positions was never the Roman way although, as Professor Jim Crow explained during the TV series, the wall was certainly capable of acting as a defensive structure.

Opposite: *Hauntingly beautiful. But what was Hadrian's Wall really for?*

BUILDING HADRIAN'S VISION

Roman army engineers faced two over-riding concerns before starting work on the wall. Where could stone be easily quarried? And, more fundamentally, would their design work in practice?

The first problem was straightforward, at least for the eastern section. The geology of the northeast typically features a hard, black, volcanic rock locally known as whinstone, interspersed with outcrops of softer sandstone and limestone. Entire legions would have grown old trying to split whinstone into building blocks and the Romans never even tried. Where possible they just incorporated the rugged crags into the line of the wall (to add height) or lobbed small chunks into the central cavity as fill material.

In contrast sandstone and limestone make ideal building material, and anyone who has visited the superbly preserved section of wall at Steel Rigg, two miles west of Housesteads Fort, can see abundant evidence of it. That's not to say the quarrying process itself was simple. The engineers would split massive boulders into smaller pieces by chiselling holes and pushing in wooden pegs soaked in water. Over time these would swell and, theoretically, split the stone along natural fissures. Unfortunately things didn't always go to plan. At Limestone Corner, near Chester's Fort, one boulder has been left in a ditch, its chisel holes clearly visible. It's not hard to imagine the site foreman swearing at it before moving on.

The second concern may seem strange given that Romans were used to large building projects and understood load-bearing and stress points. But they'd never tackled anything quite like Hadrian's Wall and perhaps weren't sure whether it would need supporting buttresses. Building a broad wall up to 3 m (10 ft) thick was considered easier than constructing a narrow one with buttressing.

That may have been the original plan but it didn't last. After a third of the length had been completed engineers decided that, after all, a narrower specification would be OK. You can clearly see this change of heart at Brunton Turret, near Chollerford, where the initial 3 m (10 ft) wide foundations laid out by advance parties lie alongside remnants of the much narrower wall actually built.

Of course the project never was built in a seamless process. Around AD 124 Hadrian decided there should be 12 permanent garrisons on the line of the wall, perhaps for 'rapid reaction' troops to handle surprise attacks. One of these is Vercovicium – *the hilly place* – better known today as Housesteads. Here we have the most complete example of a British Roman Fort including assembly hall, shrine, barracks, commander's house, hospital, operating room, granaries, stables and toilets. The toilet block is arguably Housestead's best-known building because it incorporates an innovative multi-seat latrine flushed by a drainage system which provided water for the soldiers' sponges (used instead of toilet paper).

Which brings us to the daily lives of those who served on the wall. What were their needs, hopes and fears? How did they survive on this isolated outpost of Empire? Fortunately soldiers wrote some of this down on thin wooden tablets which at one garrison were later discarded and buried under mounds of clay to create new building platforms. This sealed off the oxygen and ensured at least 1,600 tablets were preserved. The Romans couldn't have known it but they were creating one of Britain's greatest archaeological treasure chests. The ancient soap opera that was Vindolanda.

Opposite: *The architects of Hadrian's Wall used natural landscape features to bolster its defensive qualities.*

FIGHTING THE BRITONS

The dozens of forts built on or behind the wall might suggest the Romans just sat around waiting for attacks. Nothing could be further from the truth. Their commanders loved nothing better than getting some retaliation in first.

We know that the northern British tribes were a major headache for Rome because the painful memory still festered 40 years later. A letter to the Emperor Marcus Aurelius from one of Aurelius's old teachers specifically mentions Hadrian's heavy losses in Judaea and in Britain. Besides which, the location of the wall tells its own story. Why was it not built along the narrower neck of mainland between Edinburgh and Glasgow? Clearly, the Romans couldn't subdue tribes immediately south of here.

There's frustratingly little evidence about fighting around the wall, although it's unlikely that many large set-piece battles occurred. The Roman Army was 50,000 strong and if the Britons had amassed a force of any real threat then the northern auxiliary units, perhaps backed by the legions, would surely have dealt with it. The reality is that Scottish tribes fought a guerrilla war, mounting surprise attacks and retreating to the mist-covered hills. The analogy of American troops in Vietnam – 'boxers fighting the wind' – is about right.

We get a glimpse of the frustration this caused for Roman commanders in one of the Vindolanda tablets noting enemy tactics. It reads:

The Britons are unprotected by armour. There are very many cavalry. The cavalry do not use swords nor do the wretched Britons mount in order to throw javelins.

The problem is obvious: the Romans couldn't be everywhere at once. Even so, they did their best and it's clear that forts and garrisons were rarely, if ever, at full strength. Units were dispatched and seconded to other legions for specific jobs, sent on scouting missions or assigned escort duty. One Vindolanda document refers to an *arcanus* (spy), and a historian of the later empire, Ammianus Marcellinus, specifically mentions the use of spies in Britain. Their job, he wrote, was 'to circulate over a wide area and report to our generals any threatening movements among the neighbouring tribes.'

This shows that of the 752 soldiers well over half (456) were nowhere near Vindolanda. Most were at the Corbridge supply base, perhaps training for a campaign, while 46 had been seconded to the British governor's personal bodyguard, reflecting the proven loyalty of the Tungrians. The remainder may have been out patrolling, manning outpost forts or possibly conducting a tax census.

The Vindolanda strength report records only six, instead of the usual ten, centurions although below-strength units may have been the norm. All we know for sure is that on this day Vindolanda boasted a fighting force of just one centurion and 296 men. Three of the other five centurions were away leading small units on missions long lost to history.

That's the trouble with great archaeological discoveries. They unearth more questions than answers. Hadrian's Wall is at once beautiful, atmospheric and awe-inspiring – but it defends its secrets well.

Opposite: *An aerial view of Housesteads Fort, the most complete example of a Roman garrison in Britain.*

A SOLDIER'S LOT

Roman soldiers posted to Hadrian's Wall were often cold, homesick and disillusioned. Parcels from friends and family must have been eagerly awaited – with socks, underpants and beer clearly in demand.

One letter found at Vindolanda, perhaps from a soldier's mother back home on the Continent, reads: 'I have sent…you…pairs of socks from Sattua, two pairs of sandals and two pairs of underpants… Greet… Elpis… Tetricus and all your messmates with whom I pray that you live in the greatest good fortune….'

Another, sent via courier to garrison commander Flavius Cerealis, is from a cavalry officer who hints that his scouting patrol might soon return to Vindolanda for a spot of rest and relaxation. Failing that, he suggests, drinks all round wouldn't go amiss (the reference to 'king'

is a term of respect): 'Masculus to Cerialis his king, greetings. Please, my lord, give instructions on what you want us to do tomorrow. Are we all to return with the standard, or just half of us?….(missing words)…most fortunate and be well-disposed towards me. My fellow soldiers have no beer. Please order some to be sent.' It seems the import of Belgian and German beer – these were Batavian men – may be older than we think.

Belgian or not, beer was certainly cheap. The Vindolanda tablets show that 100 pints cost half a denarius, roughly half a legionary's daily wage. In today's

terms a British drinker quaffing three pints a day would get through £1,000 per month, suggesting that although the Romans were good at enforcing taxes they weren't quite as good as the House of Commons. Life on the northern frontier was however tough for pepper lovers. An unspecified amount of pepper cost two denarii, or half a legionary's weekly wage. That equates to around £225 based on today's average weekly wage figures for England. It's possible that the soldier had opened a pizza parlour in his mess; more likely that spices were a highly prized import.

Leave was a treasured luxury for the Wall cohorts, offering a chance to meet up with old messmates and comrades from past postings. Corbridge, at the eastern end of the Stanegate road, was a popular choice because of its accessibility and size. Its huge army granary stores would have been well defended with a garrison offering plenty of potential for merchants, alehouses and, no doubt, prostitutes.

Communications between Hadrian's Wall and forts along the Stanegate were excellent by standards of the day. A letter to London could be sent and returned within a fortnight and this perhaps explains why one Vindolanda soldier, Sollemnis, faked indignation in a letter to his 'brother' Paris. He writes: '...very many greetings. I want you to know that I am in very good health, as I hope you are in turn you neglectful man, who have sent me not even one letter. But I think that I am behaving in a more considerate fashion in writing to you... to you, brother... my messmate. Greet from me Diligens and Cogitatus and Corinthus and I ask that you send me the names... Farewell, dearest brother.'

Opposite: Ruins of Homesteads Roman Fort, the most northerly border of the former Roman empire.
Above: The Bath House at Chesters fort. The arched recesses may have been used to house deity symbols or, according to one theory, as storage compartments for bathers' clothes.

THE DEAL-MAKERS

Keeping the legions fed and supplied was a major logistical exercise. Fort commanders found it easier to delegate responsibility to private enterprise – and for two entrepreneurial brothers the Roman Army contract proved a nice little earner.

We know this because Vindolanda has thrown up one detailed, well preserved letter which brings to life the interaction between soldiers and local civilians. It reveals two brothers – Octavius and Candidus – who appear to be 2nd century AD wide boys dealing in anything and everything. The mention of 500 denarii for a grain contract suggests they were big players; this kind of money would have paid an auxiliary soldier for around 18 months. Similarly, the figure of 5,000 modii of grain (around 38 tons) is hardly a village bakery order although it might refer to bulkier, unthreshed ears. The brothers' Romanized names aren't really significant. No merchant would have got anywhere in life without a Roman moniker.

The letter begins:

'Octavious to his brother Candidus, greetings. The hundred pounds of sinew from Marinus, I will settle up. From the time when you wrote about this matter, he has not even mentioned it to me. I have several times written to you that I have bought 5,000 modii of ears of grain, on account of which I need cash. Unless you send me some cash, at least 500 denarii, the result will be that I shall lose what I have laid out as a deposit, about 300 denarii, and I shall be embarrassed. So, I ask you, send me some cash as soon as possible.'

The letter informs Candidus that the wagon and animal hides he wants are at Cataractonium (Catterick) and that Octavius needs a letter of authority to collect them. There is a brief mention of bad roads injuring the animals, a complaint that Tertius (whoever he is) has not credited Octavius's account with 8½ denarii and a gripe that a client introduced by a messmate of the brothers, Frontinius, has reneged on a deal.

'He [Frontinius] was wanting me to allocate some hides,' writes an aggrieved Octavius, 'and that being so was ready to give cash. I told him I would give him the hides by the Kalends of March. He decided that he would come on the Ides of January. He did not turn up, nor did he take the trouble to obtain them since he had hides. If he had given the cash I would have given him them.'

The letter closes with a jibe at a rival trader for profiteering. 'I hear that Frontinius Julius has for sale at a high price the leather ware which he bought here for five denarii apiece. Greet Spectatus and Firmus. I have received letters from Glueco. Farewell.'

While it's difficult to be certain about the brothers' position in the Roman supply chain the most credible theory is that they were civilian entrepreneurs who held a contract to supply grain to Vindolanda. Most likely, this involved dealing with the army granary at Corbridge, a few miles east. It's also possible that Candidus was in the military (and so able to instruct someone at Catterick to give hides to Octavius) while Octavius himself was not. This theory has added weight because Octavius didn't bother writing his brother's name on the back of the letter. Candidus was obviously so well known at Vindolanda it was unnecessary.

Opposite: *A reconstructed section of Hadrian's Wall.*
Below: *Vindolanda Fort has proved to be a time capsule of the Roman Army in Britain.*

VINDOLANDA THE SOAP OPERA

Vindolanda may seem like an insignificant military outpost of Rome. Yet its commander sometimes entertained the governor of Britain – a powerful figure with the ear of the Emperor – and he and his wife would have had celebrity status. Gossip, intrigue, partying and plotting were as much a part of garrison life as any battle against the barbarians.

The wooden writing tablets unearthed at Vindolanda are thought to date from between c AD 85 and AD 130. This is an obscure period of Roman occupation but we know that in AD 82/83 Agricola defeated a Scottish tribal alliance at an unknown battlefield called *Mons Graupius*. By the end of the 1st century AD the legions had withdrawn to a defensive line of forts, of which Vindolanda was one, on the 'Stanegate' Roman road linking Carlisle and Corbridge. Vindolanda therefore predates its near-neighbour Housesteads, which stands 2.5 miles east on Hadrian's Wall.

The legionaries may have built the wall but it was manned by auxiliary army units. These were recruited from conquered regions across the empire and were sometimes led by favoured tribal noblemen. Army policy prevented these 'Romanized' units serving in their own provinces, partly to discourage desertions and rebellions, and at the time the tablets were written Vindolanda was garrisoned by the ninth cohort of Batavians and the first cohort of Tungrians. Both originated from an area near modern-day Belgium.

It is the Batavian commander, the Prefect Flavius Cerialis, whose official and private business is recorded in more than 80 of the tablets. His name, though common among Romans, suggests his family gained citizenship through an act of loyalty to Titus Flavius Sabinus, otherwise known as the Emperor Vespasian (reigned AD 69–79). Perhaps Cerialis's father sided with Rome during the Batavian revolt which followed Emperor Nero's death (AD 68). Whatever his background, Cerialis must have been of 'equestrian' or wealthy social rank and he appears to have had a good relationship with the British governor Neratius Marcellus, who ruled the province around AD 103. Certainly troops from Vindolanda formed part of the governor's trusted personal bodyguard.

Cerialis' status meant his wife Sulpicia Lepidina, their children and household slaves joined him at the garrison. Judging by excavated jewellery and footwear other women (perhaps concubines of soldiers) were also present, sleeping with their children in the cramped quarters. Though in regular contact with London and other garrisons, Vindolanda was a self-contained community with its own farms, cooks, brewers, labourers and craftsmen. Social life would have revolved around religious festivals, mess parties, formal military dinners and family gatherings.

We get a glimpse of this lifestyle from one tablet written to Lepidina from her friend, Claudia Severa, wife of another commander Aelius Brocchus. Using the formal style of the Roman officer class, Claudia writes:

Claudia Severa to her Lepidina greetings. On 11 September, sister, for the day of the celebration of my birthday, I give you a warm invitation to make sure that you come to us, to make the day more enjoyable for me by your arrival, if you are present (sic). Give my greetings to your Cerialis. My Aelius and my little son send him their greetings. I shall expect you, sister. Farewell, sister, my dearest soul, as I hope to prosper, and hail.'

Opposite: *The remains of the house of a Roman military officer at Vindolanda.*

STONEHENGE

Presented by Vic Reeves

Comedian and author, Vic Reeves, provides the guided tour of this historic landmark, discovering its religious and cultural significance to our nation, and why it is still so relevant to people in the 21st century.

THE STONEHENGE ENIGMA

With traffic buzzing just 500 yards away Stonehenge by day can seem a sad,
incongruous monument to a forgotten age. But approach it in the quiet of dawn,
or the early hours of a moonlit night, and the stones somehow grow in status.
In 4,000 years their power to enchant and inspire has never failed.

It's difficult to overstate the archaeological challenges presented by Britain's – arguably Europe's – greatest piece of Bronze Age engineering. For one thing, Stonehenge was not the product of a single people and so its function may well have changed over the years. Was it a cemetery, religious temple, place of execution, astronomical computer or glorified picnic area? The answer is all of the above. Probably.

We know from radiocarbon measurements that Stonehenge was constructed in three main phases. The earliest dates from around 3200 BC when a circular 97.5m (320 ft) diameter ditch was dug encompassing an internal bank, central wooden 'sanctuary' and single entrance. The design incorporated alignments to both summer and winter solstices and extreme positions of the moon (its most southerly rising and northerly setting). Some 800 years later the cremated remains of humans – possibly ritual offerings – were sunk in 56 holes spaced around the perimeter.

The second phase began around 2200 BC. The wooden sanctuary building was replaced with two circles totalling 80 dolerite and rhyolite pillars, the celebrated bluestones which many believe were transported 240 miles from the Preseli Hills in Pembrokeshire, South Wales. Recently this theory has been questioned and some experts now think the bluestones were actually scoured from the ground by glaciers and deposited on Salisbury Plain close to the Stonehenge site. Either way, the bluestone rings were erected at the end of an 'entrance avenue' – parallel ditches aligned to the midsummer solstice. Some key 'outliers' were also raised during this period, namely the Slaughter Stone, Heel Stone and Station Stones.

During the third building phase, around 2000 BC, the bluestones were pulled down and replaced with five giant sarsen trilithons (horizontal megaliths each borne by two uprights) which today provide the monument's definitive image. Some of these bus-sized stones weigh around 50 tons and are thought to have been brought from chalk quarries on the Marlborough Downs 30 km (20 miles) to the west. At some point the Altar Stone was placed in the middle while the bluestones were recycled to form an inner horseshoe around it.

Conservative estimates suggest that these three separate building projects must have together totalled thirty million hours of manual labour. Even when this is averaged out over 1,200 years the amount of time, effort and co-operation required seems scarcely credible. The Stonehenge workforce would have needed regular food, water and shelter – a major call on primitive farmers who were effectively having to support a totally unproductive group. It certainly can't be argued that the stones helped predict the agricultural crop cycle. In southern England the summer solstice occurs long after the start of the growing season, while the winter solstice is hopelessly late for harvest.

What is clear is that Stonehenge's architects had a level of mathematical and technological sophistication which is hard to explain. At least three thousand years before Arya Bhata 'discovered' the value of Pi, they were putting similar concepts into practice.

Opposite: *In the blue light of early morning Britain's greatest Bronze Age monument is unveiled in all its majesty.*

DEATH IN THE TEMPLE

Modern-day pagans revere Stonehenge as a temple of peace and harmony, a monument to the power of nature. Yet it was also a place of execution – perhaps to dispense prehistoric justice; perhaps to offer human sacrifice.

We of course know nothing of the Bronze Age religious beliefs associated with Stonehenge. However it's clear from the hundreds of well-preserved 'bog bodies' found in peatlands across northern Europe that ritual human sacrifice was occurring as late as the Iron Age (c. 600 BC onwards). The best known example is Denmark's Tollund Man, found lying naked in the foetal position; a leather cap on his head, a belt around his waist and the rope, from which he had been hanged, still circling his neck. At Stonehenge two skeletons have been recovered which bear clear signs of execution. One,

excavated in 1978 from the ditch surrounding the stones, suggests the victim had been subjected to some kind of firing squad, his body riddled with flint-tipped arrows. For his sake it's to be hoped the arrows were fired simultaneously.

The second body was discovered in 1923 but, at the time, was not seen as particularly significant. It was thought the man, aged in his mid-30s, had died of natural causes and the skeleton ended up at the Royal College of Surgeons in London for research or reference use. When the Luftwaffe launched its bombing blitz on

London in 1941 the RCS took three direct hits which all but obliterated the building. The skeleton, it was assumed, was destroyed in the rubble.

And there the story would have ended but for the chance discovery of an old letter by an archaeologist researching material for a book. This indicated that the Stonehenge skeleton had been moved to the Natural History Museum and, sure enough, in 1999 it was found there stored, labelled and gathering dust.

Jacqueline McKinley, of Wessex Archaeology, carried out a re-examination of the bones and noticed a tiny nick on the lower jaw together with a cut mark on the fourth neck vertebra. The victim had died from a clean blow – probably a sharp sword – delivered from behind and penetrating deeply into the left of his face. This was not a typical battle injury and the use of a single grave points to a staged death. It's feasible that the victim was forced to his knees, allowing his executioner to deliver a single strike from behind. Radiocarbon dating suggests the man lived around 2,000 years ago, which places him in northern Europe's late Iron Age – long after the people who built Stonehenge. However we know the site remained in use for thousands of years and it may well have been sacred to the druids, the Celtic priests whose heyday came around the time of the Roman invasion of Britain in the mid 1st century AD. Roman propaganda certainly linked Druidism to human sacrifice and the fact that a man was executed at such an important and dramatic venue as Stonehenge suggests either a ritual killing or a desire to single him out for special punishment.

Opposite: *Sun sets over Stonehenge.*
Below: *A view of the central sarsen stone ring from the Slaughter Stone.*

THE KING OF STONEHENGE

It began as a routine excavation, a small oddly shaped Roman cemetery on land destined for a new school. The archaeologists were hoping to knock off promptly, avoiding the traffic of a busy spring bank holiday. Then amid the shards of pottery a piece of gold jewellery, possibly an earring, emerged. And suddenly everyone wanted to work late.

It had been obvious from the early stages of that 2002 dig in Amesbury, Wiltshire, that the Roman graves were dug on the site of two far earlier Bronze Age burials. There was nothing unusual in this – after all Stonehenge lay just 3 km (2 miles) to the northwest – but the size of the graves and the sheer quantity of 4,000 year-old pottery, certainly was unexpected. The discovery of the earring, swiftly followed by its pair, changed everything. Gold from this era is extremely unusual in Britain because people were only just beginning to understand metalworking and the 'magical' qualities of copper and gold.

What followed put the archaeologists in dreamland. Bronze Age graves occasionally contain the odd high-value item; this one had more than 100. As well as the 'earrings' the skeleton in the larger grave had been buried with a black sandstone archer's wrist-guard, three copper knives, metalworking tools, leather goods, bone cloak pins, a shale belt ring and dozens of beaker pots. Fifteen arrow heads were scattered over his lower body, suggesting a quiver of arrows had been emptied during the funeral ritual. Inevitably, the man was nicknamed The Amesbury Archer.

But the surprises didn't end there. Analysis of one knife showed that the metal came from Spain. The gold was mined somewhere in Europe. A forensic technique called oxygen isotope analysis, which unlocks a chemical code in tooth enamel to reveal where a person grew up, showed that the 'Archer' was born in a cold climate – possibly the Alps. Here was a man who had travelled far. Who was sufficiently revered to be accorded the richest Bronze Age grave ever discovered in Britain. Who had trade contacts across Europe. Whose metal possessions were incredibly rare. And who was buried close to the great ritual centre of Stonehenge at a time when the huge bluestones were being hauled into place. Archaeologists hate making sweeping statements but this was indisputably no ordinary archer. Judging by all known status symbols of the day, this man was a king.

Further analysis of the skeleton has produced other tell-tale hints about his life. He was powerfully built, relatively old at the time of death (35–45 years) and suffered from two horrible injuries – a bone infection caused by injury to his left knee and a tooth abscess festering in his jaw. Both would have caused foul-smelling discharges. He was a hunter and skilled metalworker, but did he come to Britain as a conqueror, emigrant or pilgrim?

The Amesbury excavation yielded one other intriguing fact during a comparison between the 'king's' skeleton and the man buried more modestly (and probably later) nearby. Both had a particular instep bone which was articulated – not a condition which they'd even notice but very unusual nonetheless. This strongly suggests the two were related, possibly even father and son. Were they the founders of Britain's first royal dynasty? And, if so, did they order the construction of Stonehenge?

Opposite: *The Stonehenge trilithons – two uprights capped with a horizontal stone – lit by a dramatic sunset.*

LEGACY OF A FREE FESTIVAL

While Stonehenge has basked in worldwide fame its two neighbouring 'cousins', Woodhenge and Durrington Walls, are often ignored by sightseers. All three are part of the same World Heritage Site and, according to new theories, may be inextricably linked to a huge prehistoric festival.

Woodhenge lies 3 km (2 miles) northeast of Stonehenge and is strikingly similar in its circular design. Constructed around 2300 BC (the end of Stonehenge's first building phase) the outer ditch and bank measure just under 76 m (83 yards) across and enclose the remnants of postholes used for timber uprights. The skeleton of a young child, its skull split open, was excavated close to the centre suggesting that ritual sacrifice may have taken place.

A mile west of Woodhenge, and 3 km (1.8 miles) north of Stonehenge, lies Durrington Walls – an enormous circular earthwork 480 m (525 yards) across. This structure was built between 3100 and 2400 BC and may for a time have accommodated Stonehenge labourers as they sweated away their days erecting stones. At one point the population reached several hundred, making it the largest known Stone Age village in Britain.

Excavations at Durrington in 1967 and 2003 show that the timber houses were around 1.5 m sq (16 ft sq) with clay floors and a central fireplace. People slept in wooden box beds – similar to a stone type found at the Skara Brae ancient village on Orkney – and appear to have had an unlimited supply of food. Among the hundreds of discarded pig bones many were only half-

eaten. Yet, curiously, there is a general lack of everyday essentials such as craft tools, hide-cleaning equipment and grinding stones.

It's this puzzle which is shedding new light on the entire Stonehenge complex. Durrington's pigs seem to have farrowed in spring and been slaughtered at nine months – bang on time for a midwinter festival. And interestingly, the site's timber posts align precisely with the midwinter solstice sunrise. As for the lack of domestic hardware, perhaps the explanation is that Durrington was occupied *only* during special winter festivals. Visitors would literally turn up, pig out and head home.

But what of a link between the three sites? For many years archaeologists have pondered the purpose of clearly defined tracks, or 'avenues' leading both from Stonehenge and Durrington Walls down to the River Avon. Professor Mike Parker Pearson, of Sheffield University, suspects these tracks were used for winter solstice funerary processions held during feasting. The dead would be transported from Durrington or Woodhenge (made of timber and representing the living) and deposited in the river to drift towards Stonehenge (aligned with the midwinter *sunset* and representing the dead). Certain high-status individuals would be granted an overland procession to Stonehenge for land burial, accounting for the hundreds of nearby barrows.

This theory has produced a spirited academic debate from which hard conclusions may never surface. All we can say with certainty is that these three great ritual centres were for thousands of years the centre of prehistoric British culture. In the soil of Salisbury Plain, their story is still unfolding.

Opposite: *Individually-sized posts give visitors an idea of Woodhenge's scale.*
Above: *A fuller reconstruction of Woodhenge at Woodbridge, North Newnton, for the TV programme* Timeteam.

THE SOLSTICE SEEKERS

On Midsummer Day Stonehenge becomes the focus of religious ceremonies for thousands of pagans and druids. They come to worship, meditate, cheer the sunrise and act out folk tales. But, mostly, they come to party…

Time was when these celebrations would involve a handful of white-cloaked druids, a few VW camper-loads of hippies and a couple of bored policemen snoozing in a patrol car. But the rise of so-called New Age beliefs, and the renaissance of pagan Britain's 'Old Religion', has turned the summer solstice at Stonehenge into a mega-festival for 23,000 people. Handily, it tends to coincide with the bi-annual open-air rock concert 80 km (50 miles) west at Glastonbury.

The build-up to that climactic moment when the sun rises above the Heel Stone (the earliest time is 4.58am) is almost as good as the moment itself. The crowd is an eclectic mix of druids in flowing white robes, pagan wedding guests, blokes dressed as wizards and virtually the entire West Country therapy and healing industry. Few though can beat the sheer theatre proffered by King Arthur Pendragon, head battle chieftain of the British Council of Druids.

Mr Pendragon, a former parliamentary candidate for Winchester incidentally, leads a troop of warriors in a dance to honour the natural order of things. In 2005 the 'warriors' turned out to be anthropology students from the University of East London, although in fairness this didn't affect their enthusiasm for holding aloft

an effigy of Mother Nature illuminated by blazing torches. Mr Pendragon says the solstice is all about commemorating the defeat of the mythical Oak King, who rules the first half of the year, in battle with the Holly King, who rules the second.

Before 2000, when English Heritage finally opened Stonehenge at Midsummer free of charge, there were a few unseemly scenes. Many pagans took exception to police restricting access to pre-registered groups and on at least one occasion a pitched battle took place. Since then solstice events have been far more orderly affairs, although the occasional tensions still surface.

The Midwinter solstice is particularly important for pagans as it represents the start of a new growing cycle in which the sun is re-born from the depths of darkness. There was some confusion in 2006 when the actual moment of solstice – the mid-point of the longest night – fell at 22 minutes past midnight on December 22nd. English Heritage wanted pagans to turn up at 7.45am

later that morning but at least 60 arrived 24 hours early believing, not unreasonably, that by 7.45 they would have missed the action, so to speak. It would never have happened in 2000 BC.

While Stonehenge is the 'honeypot' attraction for tourists visiting Salisbury Plain it's worth mentioning that another iconic symbol of Britain, which also claims a long and rich religious heritage, lies right on its doorstep. Salisbury Cathedral, topped by England's tallest spire 123 m (404 feet), dates from 1220 and is one of twenty cathedrals built by the Normans. It contains 70,000 tonnes of stone, 3,000 tons of timber and 450 tons of lead yet, incredibly, has foundations just 1.2 m (4 feet) deep.

Opposite: *The celebrations begin at Midsummer sunrise.*
Above left: *A priest performs pagan rituals.*
Above right: *The architectural triumph and majesty that is Salisbury Cathedral.*

LIVING WITH THE STONES

During World War I an author called Edith Olivier was driving from Devizes to Marlborough in Wiltshire when she stopped for a break at Avebury. Music was coming from within the stone circle enclosing half the village and lights shone in the gathering dusk. Miss Olivier assumed a fair was taking place.

Later that evening in Marlborough, 10 km (6 miles) away, she remarked on the celebrations. She was assured that Avebury hadn't hosted a fair in half a century and that she must have been mistaken. Miss Olivier later recalled the experience in her book *Without Knowing Mr Walkley*, concluding that she'd experienced 'hindsight'. Given that she later claimed to have seen the lost land of Lyonesse from Land's End, it's easy to dismiss her claim as the rantings of a lonely spinster. And yet, as anyone who has visited Avebury knows, there is a sense of timelessness about the place.

What we can say for certain is that Avebury ranks alongside the Stonehenge complex 32 km (20 miles) south as an outstanding prehistoric monument. Dating from around 2600 BC it originally contained about 100 stones and covered an area of 11.5 ha (28½ acres), contained within an outer circular ditch and chalk bank. The 40-tonne stones were quarried from Marlborough Downs and painstakingly hauled overland, most probably on wooden rollers, an astounding feat when you consider that most of Stonehenge's megaliths are only half that weight.

Sadly, only 27 stones still stand. Some were buried inside the circle during the 14th century while others were broken up using fire and hammers in response to suggestions that Avebury conducted the Devil's business. Villagers may or may not have believed this but took the pragmatic approach and used the fragments to build houses. Their efforts can still be seen in some of the walls.

Nonetheless, the grandeur of Avebury has not been entirely lost. The main circle contains two smaller ones of 96 m (320 ft) and 104 m (340 ft), each planned with a central setting or 'altar'. There are four entrances and an avenue of stones leading towards Overton Hill, 2.4 km (1.5 miles) away. Some archaeologists think this may have represented the body of a snake, the Avebury circle being its head, and that the use of alternate tall, thin stones and broader trapezoidal ones had a male and female theme. But because nobody has a clue what went on at Avebury, these theories are little more than informed speculation. It seems likely though that the circle's function is linked to the nearby 40 m (130 ft) high Silbury Hill, Europe's largest man-made mound, constructed around the same point in time.

The labour force required to produce structures such as these is truly mind-boggling. Avebury's ditch was 9 m (30 ft) deep – higher than a two-storey house, though it has since silted up – and an estimated 4 million cubic feet of chalk was removed and banked up to form a 7.5 m (25 ft) high ditch. This was achieved using workers whose only tools appear to have been picks made from discarded deer antlers. Once complete, the bank would have shone brilliant white for miles around.

Miss Olivier's twilight fair may have been the stuff of fiction but she's not alone in reporting strange events at Avebury. According to folklore small figures can sometimes be seen moving between the stones in the moonlight and the Diamond Stone, near the northwest entrance, is said to cross the road at midnight.

Opposite: *Avebury's circle once contained 100 stones.*
Below: *Silbury Hill is Europe's largest man-made mound.*

TAKE A VIEW

NEWCASTLE

HIKE IT
Walk the north bank of the Tyne along the 8 km (5 mile) Waterside Trail. You can start from Royal Quays, North Shields, head out to the ruined priory at Tynemouth, then turn north along the coastal beaches to St Mary's Island lighthouse. It's flat going, peppered with pubs and a Metro station is never far away.

BIKE IT
Newcastle is part of the North Sea Cycle Route and appears on Route 72 of the National Cycle Network. It also links to Rivers Way and Coast and Castles cycle routes and offers off-road detours for the more adventurous.

WIDER VIEW
Take a trip south of the Tyne to the Bowes Railway at Springwell Village, Gateshead. There are some 19th century colliery buildings here where blacksmiths and wheelwrights can be seen in action. There's also some wonderfully preserved rolling stock, mostly restored, on site.

ONLINE VIEW
- Tourism enquiries – Newcastle Council www.newcastle.gov.uk
- Gateshead Council www.gateshead.gov.uk
- Tanfield Railway www.tanfield-railway.co.uk
- Durham Mining Museum www.dmm.org.uk
- Swan Hunter shipyard www.swanhunter.com
- The Sage www.thesagegateshead.org/
- BALTIC Centre for Contemporary Art www.balticmill.com/

BLACKPOOL

HIKE IT
To get a taste of the countryside, choose Marton Mere Nature Reserve from Stanley Park via the Woodland Gardens and Heron's Reach. For the less ambitious try Blackpool Model Village and Gardens.

BIKE IT
Blackpool is on National Cycle Network 62 and the council has a bike-friendly strategy that includes three excellent urban tourist routes – the Jubilee, Talbot Square and Starr Gate to South Pier.

WIDER VIEW
Lytham St Annes is just around the corner but has an entirely different atmosphere to Blackpool. Going further afield, head for Preston through the Ribble Valley or Lancaster with its splendid castle.

ONLINE VIEW
- Blackpool Pleasure Beach www.blackpoolpleasurebeach.com
- Blackpool Tower www.theblackpooltower.co.uk
- Blackpool tourism www.visitblackpool.com
- Live shows www.blackpoollive.com
- Blackpool Council www.blackpool.gov.uk

SEVEN SISTERS

HIKE IT
Seven Sisters Country Park has two well marked routes – the 5-km (3-mile) Park Trail and the 8-km (5-mile) Habitat Trail – either of which will see off that long Sunday pub lunch. Both trails begin at the gate opposite the Visitor Centre.

BIKE IT

Serious mountain bikers will want to try the South Downs Lemming Trail – 160 km (100 miles) and 2,743 m (9,000 ft) of mainly off-road climbs which can allegedly be completed in two days. The South Downs Way is slightly easier and the breathtaking views make all that huffing and puffing worthwhile.

WIDER VIEW

Travelling west out of Brighton there is the grand fortification of Arundel and the pretty city of Chichester in swift succession for motorists. Roman historians will find Bignor Villa and Fishbourne Palace irresistible while 17th century Petworth House forms the northerly point of this triangle.

ONLINE VIEW

- Brighton & Hove City Council – www.brighton-hove.gov.uk
- The Royal Pavilion www.royalpavilion.org.uk
- Seven Sisters Country Park www.sevensisters.org.uk
- National Trails – South Downs Way www.nationaltrail.co.uk
- South Downs Joint Committee www.southdownsonline.org

LONDON

HIKE IT

The 'Walk This Way' routes offer four heritage trails of around 5 km (3 miles) taking in major sights around the Thames Path. The routes are Golden Jubilee Bridges, Millennium Bridge, Riverside London and South Bank.

BIKE IT

Order yourself a free copy of the London Cycling Guide (0845 305 1234) which contains 19 designated routes around the heart of the city. By 2010 the London Cycle Network Plus will offer 900 km (560 miles) of marked roads and paths.

WIDER VIEW

Try Greenwich Palace, Hampton Court Palace and Windsor Castle for history, Highgate Cemetery for atmosphere and Walthamstow market, the longest daily street market in Europe, for shopping if your budget doesn't extend to Bond Street.

ONLINE VIEW

- London tourism www.visitlondon.com
- Historic Royal Palaces www.hrp.org.uk
- Mayor of London www.london.gov.uk
- Walk This Way www.southbanklondon.com/walk_this_way
- London Cycling Campaign www.lcc.org.uk

BATH

HIKE IT

There's the Bath City Trail marked with pavement plaques in addition to a further five 'Heritage and Country Walks' in rural and urban settings, all accessible by public transport. A pack of route cards costs £2.50 + £1 p&p from Bath TIC who can also advise on the world's first Texting Trail – guidance by mobile phone.

BIKE IT

The Kennet & Avon Cycle Route is a popular waterside cycle route, starting at Bristol Temple Meads stations and stretching for 64 km (40 miles) into distant Devizes. Initially, the route follows the Bristol to Bath Railway Path through the Avon Valley, a pioneering traffic-free cycle path which set the standard for the National Cycle Network (Route 4). After Bath, where the canal begins, cycling is permitted throughout the length of the waterway.

WIDER VIEW

It's a World Heritage City but there's lots more to see in the region, including neighbouring city Bristol, the Cotswolds and the Mendips. Watch out too for Solsbury Hill, made famous by the Peter Gabriel song, and the Dundas aqueduct.

ONLINE VIEW

- Bath Tourism www.visitbath.co.uk
- Bath & North East Somerset council www.bathnes.gov.uk
- Jane Austen Centre www.janeausten.co.uk
- Roman Baths www.romanbaths.co.uk
- Bath Fringe Festival www.bathfringe.co.uk

CO. DOWN

HIKE IT

Follow the footfall of Saint Patrick from his landing place on the shores of Strangford Lough near Raholp, around the coastline to Newcastle on the Lecale Way, although it will take several days to complete.

BIKE IT
Strangford Lough

There's a circular route from the Tourist Information Centre in Newtownards that takes in Mount Stewart, the Ards peninsula, Portaferry, Ilclief Castle and Downpartrick. Not for the fainthearted.

ONLINE VIEW

- Down District Council www.downdc.gov.uk
- Newry and Mourne District Council www.newryandmourne.gov.uk
- St Patrick Centre www.saintpatrickcentre.com
- Walk Northern Ireland www.walkni.com
- Outdoor Ireland (North) for walking and cycling www.outdoorirelandnorth.co.uk

EDINBURGH

HIKE IT

Do a ghost walk in Edinburgh at night or take a coastal walk along the Firth of Forth by day. There are plenty of other walks too using disused railway lines, notably the Water of Leith Walkway. And don't neglect the extinct volcanoes that crop up around the city as they are surprisingly wild given their urban location.

BIKE IT

East of Edinburgh, visit Haddington and North Berwick by bike using abandoned railway lines that form a comprehensive cycleway.

WIDER VIEW

North Berwick is a fading Edwardian resort that offers boat trips in clement weather. In the other direction Linlithgow has a fine palace closely associated with Mary, Queen of Scots, that's open to the public. There are good public transport links to Glasgow.

ONLINE VIEW

- Edinburgh tourism www.edinburgh.org
- City council www.edinburgh.gov.uk
- Edinburgh Fringe Festival www.edinburgh.org/events/edinburgh_festival
- Edinburgh Guide www.edinburghguide.com
- Water of Leith walk www.waterofleith.edin.org

ISLE OF SKYE

HIKE IT

Coire na Creiche and the Fairy Pools circuit takes in the Cuillan scenery without walkers crossing the pain barrier. Lasting for 8 km (5 miles), it starts from the car park in Glen Brittle, accessible by the 53 bus from Portree. Check the Skyewalk website for a detailed route.

BIKE IT

Hire a bike at Portree if you want to cycle around the hills of Skye. Few of the inclines are difficult except perhaps for the slopes associated with Staffin. Weight of traffic on the A87 is linked to the ferries at Uig so check out the ferry times to plan a quiet run on the 16 km (10 mile) section south from Uig.

WIDER VIEW

Don't miss any of the islands, including small ones like Rum and Eig or the larger archipelago of Harris and Lewis. After landing on Lewis include Calanais (Callanish) on your tour, where fascinating monoliths have dominated for untold centuries.

ONLINE VIEW

- Scottish Tourism www.visitscotland.com/
- Dunvegan Castle www.dunvegancastle.com
- Skye bird watching www.skye-birds.com
- Walking on Skye www.skyewalk.co.uk
- Scottish climbing www.scotclimb.org.uk

YORKSHIRE DALES

HIKE IT

Both beautiful and surprisingly undemanding, the Dales Way links Yorkshire and Cumbria's National Parks. Officially it starts at Ilkely but there are spurs heading into Leeds, Bradford and Harrogate. Even if you start in a city you will quickly end up in spectacular countryside on this major route, opened in the 1980s. Don't expect to do it all in a day, though, for it extends at least 129 km (80 miles).

BIKE IT

Starting at Asygarth Falls an 17 km (11 mile) circular cycle path called 'A Wander in Wensleydale' takes in Carperby, Askrigg and Thorton Rust.

WIDER VIEW

There's plenty at Bolton Abbey, including a ruined priory and a steam railway although it's probably worth pushing on to Fountains Abbey if it's monastic ruins you are after. Meanwhile Harrogate remains one of the most elegant of Yorkshire towns.

ONLINE VIEW

- North Yorkshire County Council www.northyorks.gov.uk
- Yorkshire Dales National Park www.yorkshiredales.org.uk
- Dales cycle routes www.cyclethedales.org.uk
- Skipton Castle www.skiptoncastle.co.uk
- Bolton Abbey www.boltonabbey.com

THE GOWER

HIKE IT

Tap into local knowledge with the book *Walking Around Gower* from the West Glamorgan Ramblers Association, including 10 different walks. Alternatively, download walks from the website run by the National Trust, which owns three quarters of the Gower.

BIKE IT

Choose the Clyne Valley, traffic free and scenic, starting at Blackpill and meandering through the Clyne Valley Country Park.

WIDER VIEW

Heading west from the Gower there's the National Botanic Gardens of Wales close to the market town of Camarthen. Further still there's the charming resort of Tenby, and the visual delights of Pembrokeshire.

ONLINE VIEW

- National Trust www.nationaltrust.org.uk
- Countryside Council for Wales www.ccw.gov.uk

- CADW – Welsh Historic Monuments - www.cadw.wales.gov.uk
- Swansea Bay Tourism www.visitswanseabay.com
- Dylan Thomas appreciation website www.dylanthomas.com

ST IVES

HIKE IT
The South West is circuited by a 1,014 km (630 mile) coast path and perhaps the most challenging section lies between St Ives and Pendeen Watch. Best done in sunshine for the Atlantic views, don't forget, this part of the path is largely bereft of shelter and refreshment. So, in best Scouting tradition, be prepared!

BIKE IT
The old Mineral Tramways from Devoran to Portreath have recently become a cycleway, following rail tracks that once carried mined minerals to the ancient quays at Devoran or the harbour at Portreath.

WIDER VIEW
Go north to Newquay for night life, south to Marazion for the splendour of St Michael's Mount while to the south-west there are the coves and countryside of the Lizard peninsula.

ONLINE VIEW
- Joint Cornwall local authority site - www.cornishkey.com
- Visit Cornwall - www.cornwalltouristboard.co.uk
- Poldark tin mine - www.poldark-mine.co.uk
- Virginia Woolf Society www.virginiawoolfsociety.co.uk
- D. H. Lawrence website (University of Nottingham) www.dh-lawrence.org.uk
- Southwest Coast Path team - www.southwestcoastpath.com

LAKE DISTRICT

HIKE IT
Grab any of Alfred Wainwright's books for insightful guidance on a lakeland hike. Alternatively, walk between the mountains and the Solway Plain for a different view. Find Ireby village square and begin a 6 km (4 mile) gentle walk through the Ellen Valley taking in Aughtertree and Ruthwaite.

BIKE IT
A short family cycle ride which can be extended by tacking on the Hawkshead Moor route. For the fitter cyclist, there's the 16-km (10-mile) North Face mountain bike trail.

WIDER VIEW
There's not much outside the National Park that can match the Lakes for scenery but Kendal, home of the mint cake, is nonetheless a pleasant market town. St Bees on the coast is ancient and wild, marking the start of Wainwright's coast-to-coast walk which ends at Robin Hood's Bay.

ONLINE VIEW
- Cumbria tourism www.golakes.co.uk
- Wordsworth Trust www.wordsworth.org.uk
- Kendal Museum www.kendalmuseum.org.uk
- Museum of Lakeland Life www.lakelandmuseum.org.uk
- Abbot Hall art gallery www.abbothall.org.uk

NORTHUMBRIA

HIKE IT
In north Northumbria lies Kielder Water, the largest man-made lake in Europe. The surrounding forest, one of Britain's biggest nature resorts, is home to red squirrels, deer and birds of prey. There are several

well-marked trails around its 43 km (27 mile) waterline that take in history, views and nature.

BIKE IT
Part of Route 1 of the National Cycle Network links country roads and off-road trails along 130 km (80 miles) of the Northumberland coast between Tynemouth Ferry terminal and Berwick-upon-Tweed. There are some choice locations along the way, including the castles at Warkworth, Bamburgh and Dunstanburgh, Druridge Bay Country Park and the Holy Island of Lindisfarne. Easy on the eye it is also kind to the legs as the gradients are gentle ones.

WIDER VIEW
To continue Northumbria's castle theme visit the inland fortifications of Chillingham, Etal and Norham castles. The Cheviot Hills in Northumberland National Park are also highly recommended to visitors.

ONLINE VIEW
- Coast and Castles cycling route www.coast-and-castles.co.uk
- Kielder Water website www.kielder.org
- Holy Island, Lindisfarne www.lindisfarne.org.uk/
- Bamburgh Castle www.bamburghcastle.com
- Alnwick Castle www.alnwickcastle.com

LIVERPOOL

HIKE IT
Facing up to its part in the slave trade, Liverpool has turned this blot on the landscape into an important historic marker. The walk, known as the Slavery History Trail, starts at Pier Head on Liverpool's waterfront.

BIKE IT
Regeneration in Liverpool has meant superb access for cyclists along the waterfront and around Albert Dock. It's specifically the Route 56 Waterfront section that appeals. However, beware of cycle path closures caused by on-going building work.

WIDER VIEW
You could visit Manchester, which has a host of cultural sites worth visiting. But don't tell anyone in Merseyside beforehand as the two cities are historically arch competitors, both in football and industry. Less controversially, there's Chester, a shopping centre enhanced by its delightful architecture.

ONLINE VIEW
- City Council www.liverpool.gov.uk
- Museums www.liverpoolmuseums.org.uk
- Tourism www.visitliverpool.com
- The Beatles In Liverpool www.visitbeatlesliverpool.com
- Arts listings artinliverpool.com

HADRIAN'S WALL

HIKE IT
Get your walking boots on for the Hadrian's Wall Path National Trail, no less than 134.5 km (84 miles) in length following the route of this Roman boundary that would take a minimum of four days to complete. Mostly it's in rough country although some parts touch Newcastle and Carlisle. The wall is a fragile ancient monument so walkers are requested to take a circular path and choose drier months to reduce damage underfoot, to use public transport and to stick to permitted routes.

BIKE IT
In addition to the wall, there's a diverse range of other attractions for the cyclist. Hadrian's Cycleway is a new long distance National Cycle Network Route (Number

72) which opened in July 2006.

WIDER VIEW

The wall is already strung out across the neck of Britain but to the north there's Gretna Green and the Border Forest Park while to the south lies Carlisle, a bustling heritage city, and the famously detailed open air museum at Beamish.

ONLINE VIEW AND CONTACTS

- Hadrian's Wall official website www.hadrians-wall.org
- National Trail www.nationaltrail.co.uk/hadrianswall
- Vindolanda Fort www.vindolanda.com
- Chesters Walled Garden www.chesterswalledgarden
- Northumberland Tourism www.northumberland.gov.uk

STONEHENGE

HIKE IT

A walking map for Salisbury and Wilton with 15 walks of varying lengths has been published by the district council. All start from the Guildhall Square and have route direction cards. One set of walks takes in Constable's View of Salisbury Cathedral from the Town Path across Harnham watermeadows. Pick up a copy for free at Salisbury Tourist Information Centre.

BIKE IT

Salisbury is cycle-friendly with an extensive network of cycle lanes, tracks and bridleways. There are plans for the National Cyclist Network (Route 24) to run between Bath and Southampton via Salisbury and Route 45 to go from Gloucester to Salisbury via Salisbury Plain and Stonehenge.

WIDER VIEW

At Longleat there's a stately home and safari park while the cities of Bath, Bristol and Southampton are in swift striking distance. For the mystically minded, Glastonbury Tor lies directly to the west.

ONLINE VIEW

- Stonehenge www.stonehenge.co.uk
- Sheffield University Stonehenge research
- www.shef.ac.uk/archaeology/research/stonehenge
- Salisbury Cathedral www.salisburycathedral.org.uk
- Salisbury District Council tourism – www.salisbury.gov.uk
- Wiltshire County Council www.wiltshire.gov.uk

ONLINE VIEW TOP 20

- Ramblers Association www.ramblers.org.uk
- National Cycle Network co-ordinator iSustrans – www.sustrans.org.uk.
- National Parks www.nationalparks.gov.uk
- English Heritage www.english-heritage.org.uk
- Scottish National Heritage www.snh.org.uk
- Environment and Heritage Service Northern Ireland www.ehsni.gov.uk
- CADW (Welsh heritage site) www.cadw.wales.gov.uk
- National Association for Areas of Outstanding Natural Beauty www.aonb.org.uk
- Department for Culture Media and Sport www.culture.gov.uk
- Natural England www.naturalengland.org.uk
- Open Access Countryside www.countrysideaccess.gov.uk
- British Waterways www.britishwaterways.co.uk
- Forestry Commission http://www.forestry.gov.uk
- Wildlife Trusts www.wildlifetrusts.org
- Marine Conservation Society www.mcsuk.org
- Ordnance Survey www.ordnancesurvey.co.uk
- Met Office www.metoffice.gov.uk
- British Museum www.thebritishmuseum.ac.uk
- National Maritime Museum http://www.nmm.ac.uk

INDEX

PICTURE ACKNOWLEDGEMENTS

The publishers would like to acknowledge and thank the following for
providing photographs for publication in this book.

Alamy /AA World Travel Library 104, 105, 120-121, 131 right; Mike Abrahams 198; Steve Allen Travel Photography 188; AM Corporation 169; David Bagley 130, 213; Peter Barritt 159; BL Images Ltd 8-9 & 20; Kevin Britland 152, 158; Simon Brown 89; Marion Bull 127 bottom; Adam Burton 134-135 & 140; James Cheadle 68, 229 left; Neale Clark/Robert Harding Picture Library Ltd 97; Ashley Cooper 170; Design Pics Inc 80, 203 right; Guy Edwardes Photography 46, 64-65 & 74; Elmtree Images 70; Elvele Images 122; Laurence Fordyce/Eye Ubiquitous 208; Robert Estall Photo Agency 47; Lynne Evans 162-163; Mary Evans Picture Library 69 left; eye35.com 96; Nicholas Frost 115; Rosalie Frost 71 right; Christopher Furlong 108-109; Leslie Garland Picture Library 187; Geogphotos 214, 215; Darryl Gill 168; Chris Gomersall 116; Michael Grant 45; Simon Holdcroft 43; Peter Howard 87; Chris Howes Wild Places Photography 126; Imagina Photography 222, 223; Andrew Jankunas 203 left; Kateworn images 113; Mike Kipling Photography 16, 123; landscape stock 145; Justin Leighton 101; Ian Leonard 227; Barry Lewis 27; Pawel Libera 55; Paul Lindsay 78-79 & 85; Andrew Lindscott 131 right; Liquid Light 229 right; Guillem Lopez 100; Manor Photography 225; Marshall Ikonography 220; Navin Mistry 179; Robert Morris 30; Dylan McBurney 86; Gareth McCormack 90; nagelestock.com 58, 106-107 & 114; Patrick Nairne 129; Gavin Newman 127 top; Eric Nathan 52; Alan Novelli 190-191 & 202; Andrew Paterson 226;

Graeme Peacock 12, 13, 21 right, 181; Photolibrary Wales 138, 139 right, 141, 180; Nicholas Pitt 63; Radius Images 118-119; Ben Ramos 160; Robert Harding Picture Library Ltd 171 right, 174; David Robertson 186; Rough Guides 139 left; Ruud van Ruitenbeek 128; Scottish Viewpoint 112; Malcolm Sewell 21 left, 173; Keith Shuttlewood 110; Skyscan Photolibrary 171 left, 211; Gary Smith 4-5, 111 bottom; Trevor Smithers ARPS 231; Jon Sparks 166; David Speight 132; Nigel Stollery 182; Derek Stone 36-37 & 48; Mark Sunderland 69 right; Andy Sutton 204-5; Glyn Thomas 54; Paul Thompson Images 197; Travel Ink 88; Up The Resolution (uptheres) 71 left; Darryl Webb 83; **Britain on View** /Martin Brent 11; **Corbis** /Andrew J G Bell/Eye Ubiquitous 29 left; Marco Cristofori/Zefa 103; Gillian Darley/Edifice 18; Robert Estali 207; Chinch Gryniewicz 146; Gavin Hellier 111 above; E O Hoppé 14; Robert Estall 207; Vittoriano Rastelli 94; Jon Sparks 22-23 & 29 right; Alan Towse/Ecoscene 28; Sandro Vannini 216; Steven Vidler/Eurasia Press 92-3, 218-9; Patrick Ward 34-35, 212; **Getty Images** 42, 53 left, 56, 155, 194, 200; Peter Adams 67, 144; Anders Blomqvist 230; John Chillingworth 84; Gary Cook 185; Joe Cornish 125; Rob Cousins 153; Ary Diesendruck 62; W and D Downey 136; Lee Frost 40-41, 176-177 & 189; Tim Graham 95; John Lamb 39; Lester Lefkowitz 57; Harvey Lloyd 98; Peter MacDiarmid 228; Haywood Magee/Hulton Archive 143; David Noton 6-7, 154; John Pratt 199; Ed Pritchard 2-3, 60-61; Roy Rainford 77, 165; Walter Rawlings 53 right; Ronald Startup 24; Robert Stiggins 167; Paul Thompson 192-193; Travelpix Ltd. 50-51,148-149 & 156; **Lebrecht Music & Arts Photo Library** 73; **Photolibrary Group** /Imagesource 76, 151; **Topfoto** 17 left and right.